Living Evangelism

Living Evangelism

**Affirming Catholicism
and Sharing the Faith**

Edited by
JEFFREY JOHN

Introduced by
RICHARD HOLLOWAY

DARTON·LONGMAN + TODD

First published in 1996 by
Darton, Longman and Todd Ltd
1 Spencer Court
140–142 Wandsworth High Street
London SW18 4JJ

ISBN 0–232–52166–2

A catalogue record for this book is available
from the British Library

Phototypeset by Intype London Ltd
Printed and bound in Great Britain
by Page Bros, Norwich

Contents

Notes on Contributors

JOHN HABGOOD was formerly Archbishop of York.

RICHARD HOLLOWAY is Bishop of Edinburgh and Primus of the Episcopal Church in Scotland.

JEFFREY JOHN is Vicar of Holy Trinity, Eltham, and formerly Dean of Magdalen College, Oxford.

MICHAEL MARSHALL, formerly Bishop of Woolwich, is the Archbishops' Adviser on Evangelism.

JOHN MOSES is Provost of Chelmsford.

DAVID STANCLIFFE is Bishop of Salisbury.

MARY TANNER is Secretary of the Board of Mission and Unity at Church House.

ANGELA TILBY is a writer, television producer and broadcaster.

ROWAN WILLIAMS is Bishop of Monmouth.

Introduction*

Richard Holloway

Some years ago I read an interesting book written by David Edwards, then Provost of Southwark Cathedral. It was called *The Futures of Christianity*. He tried to gaze into several possible futures for global Christianity on the basis of an analysis of its current situation. It was written before 1989, so obviously there was no mention of the interesting situation in Eastern Europe, where, for example, Russia is seeing not only a revival of Orthodoxy but a flood of Protestant cults, many of them of an extreme fundamentalist nature. In Poland the Roman Catholic Church, which led the fight against Communism and was a focus of national aspirations, is now losing its grip on society and is a less dominant institution than it was. David Edwards pointed out some things that are fairly obvious to those of us who know even a little about global Christianity. He looked at Africa, where Christian churches seem to grow at an exponential rate, and he reminded us of the plural vigour of Christianity in the United States, where the main-line denominations have been losing numbers in recent decades, but where various versions of revivalist Christianity are growing apace and sometimes allying themselves with extreme right-wing politicians. But the part of Edwards' book that I found most interesting and challenging was his analysis of the state of Christianity in northern Europe. There are exceptions to the general pattern, such as Ireland, but the picture seems to be one of fairly consistent decline, and Edwards wonders what the future might hold for a body that helped form the very reality of Europe.

A discussion I had with Brother Roger at Taizé confirmed

*© Richard Holloway 1996

something of this analysis, as far as France is concerned. I was told that in the Diocese of Autun, where Taizé is, there has been a staggering decline in rural Catholicism and the priest who runs the Taizé parish has 36 churches to look after. The positive side was that most of the congregations were effectually and effectively being run by lay people.

We are all familiar with the drumbeat of decline that the newspapers in Britain like to sound from time to time, particularly as it affects the Church of England, but the statistics are daunting enough, even if we point out that a half-empty church is also half-full. Apart altogether from any theological or philosophical position we may take on the subject of evangelism and church growth, the statistics of decline, even though we may believe that they are dramatised by the press, do suggest that Christianity, as we know it, has a problematic long-term future in Europe. The reasons are complex. One of the paradoxes in the current position is that surveys constantly show that there is little decline in the number of people who believe in God and say their prayers. It is tempting for an intellectual like me, who has personally felt the impact of the philosophical attack upon Christianity mounted in our own era by Nietzsche, Marx and Freud, to believe that the decline of Christianity is an intellectual phenomenon and that the convincing power of secular thought has eroded it as a perspective that an intelligent and educated person can hold in our time.

I suspect that some of the people who read this book or support Affirming Catholicism will have experienced this challenge to Christianity in the same, quite personal way, so that their confidence in some aspects of Christian theology has been eroded and undermined. They will nod appreciatively as they read Angela Tilby's words in this book. I have no doubt that this is the position held by many people in certain quarters of our society, but it does not seem to be true of society as a whole where, if anything, there seems to be increasing credulity, so that the decline of Christianity results not in the adoption of a bracing atheism but in the proliferation of a whole range of alternative belief systems. What seems to be true, however, is that many people in our society, who are not necessarily hostile to faith or spirituality, see the Church as irrelevant to their own real needs and find it boring and unstimulating when they experience it. The marketising of everything in our culture has affected religion as well as everything else, and Christianity is now one brand among many in the supermarket, suffering, perhaps, from the pains of lost grandeur because once it was the only brand on sale.

Should this concern us? Does it matter if Christianity declines, or if the expressions of Christianity that nourished most of us, the broad traditional expressions of the faith, both Catholic and Reformed, are reduced to a historical residue to be replaced, in time, by a vibrant sectarianism which only serves to increase the contempt that generous minds feel for the intolerant and over-confident super-believer? There are many Christians, of course, who believe that we have a message for the nations that is saving, liberating and energising. Even if some of us have perhaps lost that fervour, however, and feel that Christianity has as much to repent of as to celebrate, and even if our own position might be described as critical Christianity, surely Christianity itself is something we believe in, however broadly interpreted, and something presumably we would like to continue.

I am aware that there are what we might call a number of theological integrities and a variety of approaches to these issues. But for most of us who are probably closer to the centre than to either of the wings that define the broad range of Christian experience, the decline of Christianity is of grave concern, not because our power base is declining or because we are losing the financial support that is essential if we are to maintain our institutional life, but because we believe that the Christian way, when followed humbly and lovingly, is a gift to humanity and that something precious will have passed away from the earth if it vanishes from our midst.

In 1988 the bishops at Lambeth launched the Decade of Evangelism. The motivation behind the Decade was as complex as anything else in the Anglican Communion. There was a feeling that the older, particularly European, expressions of Christianity had lost their self-confidence; and just as European Christianity, for better or for worse, had spread the message of Christ to other nations, so the churches of the so-called Third World, economically poor but often characterised by enormous spiritual riches, looked upon the spiritual poverty of our Church in Britain and exhorted us to renew our faith and learn to share it with others. They pointed out to us that this imperative to share the faith, to tell the good news, was not a device to reclaim a share of the spiritual market, but was intrinsic to Christianity's self-understanding. From the beginning, Christianity understood itself to be a missionary religion. I have always found certain aspects and particular theological versions of this missionary imperative repulsive, but I nevertheless recognise that from the beginning the Christian Church understood itself as having a commission to share the good news of God's gracious love as made known in Christ with the world. Whatever we make of the excesses, we are Christians in Britain because Peter and Paul took Christianity to Rome and in the fullness of time Rome sent Augustine to England and Ninian to Scotland and Ireland sent Columba. Christianity has always been handed on in this way. The question for our generation is whether we ourselves can find a way that honestly and with integrity hands on the faith to succeeding generations or whether we are part of a vanishing breed, the remains of the smile on the face of the Cheshire Cat.

So far the Decade of Evangelism has had what we might call a leavening effect on the Church in Britain. We are much more prepared to think about the Church's missionary role, to see ourselves here not only to serve others with works of love and mercy, not only to challenge the powers that be in their oppression of the poor with the prophetic word of God, and not only to be a worshipping community that acts as the world's priest, lifting up holy hands in praise and penitence. All of these things we are, but we are also called to another task. However uncomfortable some of us feel about it, we are called to the task of proclamation. Experience shows that there is a mystery of grace at work here. Since this is God's world and most people in it have a heart hunger for God, the word of God, even when spoken foolishly and stumblingly, will often find a response in the hearer in a way we ourselves can never anticipate; a connection is made, a bridge is built. This is something that preachers know well. They discover time and again that words they have uttered, sometimes almost inconsequentially, almost as an aside, have on occasions been the words used by God to comfort or challenge another human being. How are we, then, to re-equip ourselves for this task?

But what is it we are about? What is this mission that we share in? According to Scripture it begins in the heart of God, whose love for us and the world is so great that he sends signals of that love to us, in prophet and poet, through the whisperings of our own nature, through the hunger we feel for meaning and love, and, finally, in the gift of Jesus, who came to make human life more abundant and to open to us the depths of God's forgiving and empowering love.

There seem to be two models of this divine activity in Scripture and in human experience. The first, the Old Testament model (though it corresponds to abiding principles in Catholic and Orthodox Christianity), is the model of magnetism. The worshipping community, by its very worship and praise of God, attracts others into its midst, magnetises them, pulls them, sometimes almost against their will, to be a part of this mysterious yet compelling activity. The great text that celebrates this compulsive power of worship is Isaiah 2:2–3.

> In the days to come the mountain of the Temple of Yahweh shall tower above the mountains and be lifted higher than the hills. All the nations will stream to it, peoples without number will come to it; and they will say: 'Come, let us go up to the mountain of Yahweh, to the Temple of the God of Jacob that he may teach us his ways so that we may walk in his paths; since the Law will go out from Zion, and the oracle of Yahweh from Jerusalem.

In other words, our very presence in the world as a worshipping community has enormous evangelical or attractive power. This was certainly the case in the Jewish Church, which never sought to make converts, yet attracted people in the ancient world by the moral and spiritual quality of its existence. The missionary imperative calls us to be a worshipping community, but it may also call us to

5

the renewal of our worship, to an understanding of worship as belonging to God and not to us, and to a recognition that, used sensitively, it can draw people to God. These are points that are well made by David Stancliffe and Michael Marshall in this book. The centrality of worship, especially in the Catholic tradition, places us inevitably in one of those fruitful tensions that so characterise the spiritual life, between worship that is worthy, a perfect offering to God, and worship that is accessible to the men and women whom God seeks to draw into the divine life. There is no absolute and perfect balance. We know that the whole spectrum of Christian tradition ranges from worship that is accessible and almost self-explanatory, right over to the deep, almost impenetrable mystery of complex liturgy which, by its very beauty and transcendent remoteness, can touch our heart hunger for God.

I always find the worship at Taizé both instructive and powerful. It is not particularly complex, but it has an enormous sense of longing and always stirs up in me a great desire for God. One of the most powerful elements in the worship at Taizé, apart from the songs and chants, is the use of silence and darkness. Here, too, we have much to learn from one another, if we will listen. Worship by itself has enormous evangelistic power.

But it is not the only way in which God's love is found in the world. The other model of God's action is the searching model. God not only draws people, God actively searches for them. Many of Christ's parables were parables of searching: the good shepherd searching for the lost sheep; the woman sweeping the house looking for her lost coin; the servants of the king going out into the highways and byways to invite the poor to the great banquet of life. And this theme of sending, of going in search of people, is true above all of the way John, in particular, expresses the meaning of the life of Jesus Christ. He is the one who comes to us from God, bringing the good news of the kingdom. In many ways this was the new thing that Christianity brought into the religious supermarket of the Ancient World. It not only accepted worshippers who sought to join it, it went in search of them. So the Church has a task, not only of being a worshipping presence in the world, setting up a magnetic field of longing for God, but of being an agent of proclamation, a searcher for God's children, active in laying the claims of God before them.

It is important to understand something of the mystery of this evangelistic activity. It is not that we are to see ourselves as travelling salesmen with a pitch, knocking on doors, compelling people to buy our brand. That happens, of course, but the mystery of the effectiveness of evangelism is much less crass than that. Basic to the theology of evangelism is the doctrine of the prevenience of God. God is already *in* the world. The world already declares God's glory. God is the light that lightens everyone. What the preaching of the word does is to send a signal, almost like a password, to the hearts and minds of those who hunger for God so that a connection is made, there is a disclosure. We ourselves are not entirely responsible for this mysterious moment of disclosure, though we may have the privilege of being the agent through which the connection is made. This may be how we can reassure one another as we engage in evangelistic work. We do not have to be perfect (no evangelism would be done if it waited for the perfect); we do not have to have absolute confidence in our own ability to express the mystery of grace; but we do somehow have to trust that God will use us in spite of our poverty and dumbness. We are not called to be successful, only to be faithful. In a strange way the work of evangelism is itself a kind of sacrament. God takes the outward and visible, our human reality in all its muddle and longing, and uses it to express an invisible spiritual reality. The methods of evangelism (and there is no enormous mystery about any of them) are the outward and visible signs of that inward and spiritual grace which is the mark of any sacrament, but the important thing to remember is that it is God who fills the sacrament with grace and not the human functionary. I am as nervous and embarrassed in this area as anyone else, but I have become increasingly persuaded that in a strange way we are being called to trust God, not ourselves, in this work to which we are commanded.

The Affirming Catholicism Conference held at York in July 1995, the papers of which are now published in this book, was built round the theme of Catholic evangelism. Some critics would see that phrase as an oxymoron, and it is certainly true that churches in the Anglican Catholic tradition are not conspicuous for their evangelistic fervour. Affirming Catholicism believes that this must change, that we must go determinedly on mission. Apart from the fact that mission is the life of the Church, if we will not do it others will – indeed, already do. As Yeats put it, 'The best lack all conviction, While the worst are filled with passionate intensity'. Many people are being drawn into narrow and mean-spirited versions of Christianity because those are the versions that take evangelism seriously. We believe that a generous and truly Catholic evangelism is possible, and we hope that this book will help us to make a start.

1 'The Double Grip of Glory'*

Michael Marshall

Archbishop John Habgood, in his book *Confessions of a Conservative Liberal*, remarks:

> In the long term the future lies with Catholicism. It must, because only Catholic tradition is rich enough and stable enough to be able to offer something distinctive to the world without being captured by the world. But it must be a Catholicism which is true to its highest vision, and hence broad enough, hospitable enough, rooted sufficiently in sacramental reality, confident enough in its inheritance to be able to do new things, diverse enough, and yet passionately enough concerned about unity, to be genuinely universal.

So we might take as our working definition of Catholic evangelism something like: 'Nothing less than the whole Gospel for the whole person and the whole created order.'

Such an evangelism will have about it, I believe, two essential characteristics. In the first place it will be local and indigenous, and secondly it will perforce be ecumenical in the best sense. It will be local because it will take local culture and cultures seriously. To do so makes us conscious of both a continuing incarnation and a continuing Pentecost, so that we can say along with those first Pentecost observers that we also see and hear this Jesus at all times in all places and in all styles, as well as 'in our own tongues'. Evangelisation for the Catholic Christian is not a matter of trying to superimpose the Jesus of history upon all the evolving cultures to the end of time, but rather forwarding the vision of the transfigured Christ of faith who always points forward to the fullness of the cosmic Christ, who

*© Michael Marshall 1996

will gather into himself all the reordered cultures of history in the fullness of time.

Furthermore, this Catholic evangelism will also be essentially ecumenical in spirit as well as in content. With something of poetic licence, therefore, I want to draw together three apostolic witnesses to this ecumenical Catholic evangelism. They are Peter, as the churchman, and Paul, as the man of the Word, both of whom we often rightly put together – as on 29 June, but (I believe with unfortunate oversight) to the exclusion of that third distinctive witness of John, the radical, the contemplative evangelist, who must always be present to rescue the witness of Peter and Paul alike from simply mutually endorsing their own fundamentalisms. Look out, when Peter and Paul are colluding in a too cosy alliance!

I say John the radical and the contemplative, because I truly believe that Anglicanism at its healthiest has been held together by what we used to call the liberal witness. With people such as F. D. Maurice, Liddon, Charles Gore, Dean Inge, Charles Raven, I believe the liberal witness was essentially the witness of the contemplative, the mystic, and the politically radical, which is most certainly not the same as the politically correct! It brought to Anglican theology and witness that essential element of apophatic theology, so precious to the Eastern tradition. It rescued both the Evangelical witness of the word and the Catholic witness of the sacraments from an endemic idolatry, while retaining and holding together the witness of Bible, Church and reason, but always as icons and not as idols. It would be my contention that the millennium hysteria of fundamentalism requires perhaps as never before this distinctive iconoclasm of the radical and contemplative witness.

Therefore I want to conclude this introduction to my topic by pointing to Mary the Mother of the Lord as the icon of the first Catholic evangelist: Mary a good Evangelical, a good Catholic and a good Radical. (Not at all, of course, the same as saying a good Protestant, a good Roman Catholic or a good Liberal.) As a matter of fact, I think she was a good Anglican!

'Good Evangelical', because she took God at his word and was obedient to that word and could therefore commend that word to the servants at Cana of Galilee 'do whatever he tells you'. 'Good Catholic', because she enfleshes that word within her. And good radical and contemplative because she ponders that word in her heart and celebrates along with Sarah and Hannah the radical and subversive order of the coming Kingdom in which God overturns 'the mighty from their seats' and 'exalts the humble and meek' – as Mary sings in the fully orchestrated version of Hannah's song, which we in the new Israel fondly refer to as the *magnificat*.

Of course, you might well ask, as she did, 'How on earth is all this possible?' How could all or any of this be possible for the Church, the bride of Christ, today? Of course, the response is almost self-evident: only if the Holy Spirit comes upon *us* and the power of the Highest overshadows *us*, so that what is formed within the heart and soul of the Church is 'all for Jesus' and Jesus 'all in all'. (So perhaps we might also claim that she was a good charismatic – which, incidentally, is not at all the same as saying that she was a pentecostalist!)

The old adage is true for Mary as it is true for the Church: Word without the Spirit and we shall *dry up*; Spirit without the Word, as recent experience has painfully proved, and we tend to *blow up*; sacraments with neither the Word nor the Spirit, and we are in danger of being *fed up*. Only with all three is there any hope for us to *grow up* into the fullness of the stature of Christ. At its best, Catholic evangelism is strong on all three fronts.

Three Theological Characteristics of Catholic Evangelism

A NEW WORLD VIEW

'In the year that King Uzziah died', records the layman Isaiah, 'I saw the Lord.' It was nothing less than that vision in the temple which constituted the mandate for universal mission. The Catholic witness within the Church of England is in dire need of recovering such a vision for its evangelism – a vision which begins in the temple but which is fulfilled with the missionary mandate: 'Who will go for

11

us and whom shall we send?' 'Lord, here am I, send me.' The vision for mission for us is focused in the celebration of the Eucharist, which also ends with the missionary mandate: 'Go in peace to love and serve the Lord.' One might almost say that the mass *is* mission: when the worship is ended the service begins! At the heart of that vision in the temple of Isaiah is the amazing and subversive disclosure: 'Holy, holy, holy is the Lord of hosts.' Nothing new or startling in that for a good Jew, or indeed a Christian, you might well say. The glory of God revealed in the temple of God was the heart and soul of the Jewish religion. But then comes the amazing disclosure: 'The whole earth is full of his glory.' This is what I like to call 'the double grip of glory' or, to use the well-known phrase of Gerard Manley Hopkins, 'the world charged with the glory of God'. Or the witness of our own George Herbert: 'Teach me my God and King in *all* things Thee to see.'

For at the heart of Catholic theology is this deep conviction from the prologue of John's gospel that 'all things were made by Him and without Him was not anything made that was made'; that Christ the Logos is the light which enlightens every man, all cultures, Greek and Jew, Christian believer and unbeliever, as well as adherents of other faiths and none. Likewise with Peter's vision at Joppa. There Peter learned that both by reason of the creation as well as of the incarnation, it is no longer proper to call anything profane, and certainly not in the literal meaning of that word. Both the Gnostic and non-sacramental perversions of Christianity have constantly declared that certain things (notably money, sex, the body) are in the profane category, only suitable to be carried out *pro-fano* – 'in front of the temple' and not *in* the temple. Hence the schizoid world of Manicheism and Calvinism.

It is significant that as Augustine stumbled around the supermarket of religious options in his day (an age not entirely dissimilar to our own), that when he stumbled upon Catholic Christianity, he made this important statement: 'I no longer desired a better world, because I was thinking of creation as a whole; and in the light of this more balanced discernment, I had come to see that higher things are better than the lower, but that the sum of all creation is better than the higher things alone' (*Confessions*, *VII*, xiii, 19). Catholic evangelism is in business for nothing less than the sum total of all creation, solemnly, yet joyfully, bent upon that gloriously apostolic task of gathering up the precious 'fragments that remain, so that nothing is lost'.

So, for example, we all know the pulpit story of the little boy who threw a stone through the window of the local church. It went straight through the letter 'E' in the gloriously displayed words: 'Glory to God in the highest', which now felicitously read: 'Glory to God in the high st.' It is that double grip of glory of Isaiah's vision which can re-envision the Church for mission. It begins with that vision – a right way of seeing the whole of God's world. It is precisely what Christ upbraids us for *not* doing – in effect, for our blindness – in Matthew, chapter 25. 'But Lord, when did we ever see you in prison or hospital?' 'I tell you, in as much as you did or did not do it for these you did or did not do it to me.' We are called to discern Christ's hidden presence and activity. So the contemplative Christian, according to Shakespeare, is to be one of 'God's spies' – one of God's undercover, subversive agents, uncovering and recovering the glory of God in the world, in the market-place as well as in the sanctuary.

John Saxbee, in his important book *Liberal Evangelism*, legitimately criticises both Evangelical, as well as many forms of Catholic evangelism, for just this blindness.

> In a large department store you can choose whether to use the stairs or take the lift when making your way from floor to floor. . . . The user of the lift, like many religious conservatives, inhabits a secure and unchanging environment, while on the stairs we see the theological liberals struggling to come to terms with each new department. . . . As we near the end of the twentieth century, more and more people are being encouraged to take the safe and secure 'lift' of Christian conservatism – with the operators not so much telling the lift occupants what is available from floor to floor as telling the floor staff what is available in the lift.

A proper vision for Catholic evangelism which takes both the creation and the incarnation seriously will not be ashamed to be captivated by the world's rich store that is stuffed with his glory – albeit ambivalent, hidden, disguised, flawed, broken and a poor likeness to the original. 'God's spies' should surely never fear contamination from the merchandise on any floor, including the basement, finding the lift too claustrophobic by half. For no matter how much religious conservatives speak of outreach, they nearly always imply (however subtly) that sort of 'draw-bridge' mentality which is only prepared for outreach providing it results in a large intake into the safety zone of the Church.

Both the vision of Isaiah and Peter's vision at Joppa give us that mandate for mission and evangelism which seeks value in all that is on offer – a value for its own sake, or rather for the sake of Him who created it in the first place. Only so are we able to transcend that schizoid view of the universe which would hold in antithesis the Gospel and the social gospel, the sanctuary and the High Street.

THE KINGDOM OF GOD, THE CHURCH AND THE GOSPEL OF CHRIST

Now is the time to play a little ecclesiastical Myers Briggs game! Forgive me if I begin by making the obviously absurd assumption that there are three types of Christians today to be found within and across all the various traditions. In group one there are those who would appear to want the King without the Kingdom; then there are those who seem to assume that you could have the Kingdom without the King; and in the third group are those who are tempted to assume that the Church *is* the Kingdom.

The first group can be found among Evangelicals, Catholics and charismatics alike. They are the pietists who love Jesus, and I have much to learn from them on that front; but they have failed to see that in the New Testament any surrender to Jesus Christ as Saviour and Lord immediately sets us to work for His Kingdom.

Those in the second group also have much to teach someone like myself. They have a passion for justice and peace; they care for the poor and work for the abolition of poverty and slavery; their song is the *magnificat* of Mary but they often give the impression that the Kingdom will come on earth within history, and that you can have the

Kingdom without surrender to the King. People like me tend to dismiss people like that as 'liberals'.

The third kind is my own camp, which I readily confess and acknowledge (though not to my credit, I fear). We are tempted to equate the Church with the Kingdom, and our evangelism is affected by such an oversimplification. The dynamic of that sort of evangelism seems to be concerned primarily with emptying the world into the Church. We may speak of bridge-building, outreach and so on, but the goal (and make no mistake about it) is to rescue everyone from the life of a depraved world, and to initiate them into what they will soon begin to describe as 'church life'.

In the sixties there was much talk of the Church taking its agenda from the world. Today there is a reaction in some quarters which would seek to redress that error with another error, namely, hoping that the world will take its agenda from the Church. A plague on both your houses! In reality both the world and the Church need to take their agenda from the Kingdom. Then, and only then, the whole dynamic of evangelism is radically changed. We do not seek to empty the world into the Church, but rather there is a self-emptying of the Church – a kenosis – into the world, pouring ourselves into the world, in order that the chemistry of a spirit-filled Church *together* with a reordered world may in God's good time be emptied into the Kingdom, that new creation which is beyond both Church and world. Both the Jesus of history and the Christ of faith herald that Kingdom as a sign of contradiction, as a counter-culture, as aliens in a foreign land. In the divine meantime our task as a Church is to pour ourselves into God's world and to celebrate the emerging new creation, against all the odds!

I hesitate to use the contemporary term 'counter-culture', precisely because it could suggest a ghetto mentality. I prefer the three positive Christ-given analogies: Christians as salt, light and leaven, respectively bringing out the flavour, illuminating and highlighting the creation in all its shadows as well as its brightness, and in and through it all, raising up the coming new creation. The Christian Church, still lame, wounded, sinful and fragmented, nevertheless by grace points through its very weakness to that

15

new quality of life; local communities of faith, living the lifestyle of the Kingdom and praying the prayer of the Kingdom, will herald, in actions which speak far louder than words, a lifestyle which is at one and the same time both *engaged* with the wider community, while remaining *distinctive* from it. Lesslie Newbigin can thus rightly claim: 'The only hermeneutic of the gospel is a congregation of men and women who believe it and live by it.'[1] For as Jesus says: 'I have come that they might have life and have it in all its fullness,' or in the often-quoted words of Irenaeus, from the end of the second century: 'The glory of God is a human being fully alive, and the life of humanity consists in the glory of God.'

Those fragile little communities of faith which we call the Church, living in the world but not of it, are in reality, I believe, at the coal face of history. However, if they are to be true to the full Catholic Gospel of the Kingdom, they must be both prophetic as well as pastoral, recalling the world through a life of contemplative prayer and radical action (and the two belong together, as they always have) to the lifestyle of that coming Kingdom, witnessing as a sign of contradiction, to resurrection even in the midst of death and decay; celebrating their story – precisely by being at all times and in all places a Church on the move in pilgrimage and passion. It is by telling our story and celebrating our story that we recover and discover our true identity as God's people, for celebration and proclamation go hand in hand.

In such a view of Catholic evangelism, the lifestyle of the whole people of God will prove to be a far more compelling witness than the rhetoric of the expensively suited and imported evangelist. I am not saying that there is no longer a place for the evangelistic rally, but I suspect that as such they will never again hold the lion's share of all that we mean by Catholic evangelism.

Rather, as salt, light and leaven, the community of faith will act out parables of the Kingdom and in so doing will automatically invite *metanoia*, that change of outlook or change of mind which repentance implies. True vision will always evoke repentance and *metanoia*. In the initial message of Jesus in Mark's gospel, as in John the Baptist's message, repentance is the hinge on which all else turns. 'The time is fulfilled; the kingdom of heaven is breaking in: repent, and believe in the gospel.' So also for Isaiah in the temple, vision came first; likewise for Job in that moment of divine disclosure in the midst of his wound of knowledge; and so again for Peter at the lake-side with the massive catch of fishes in Luke's gospel. Each encounter leads to *metanoia*.

Yet I suspect that in Catholic as well as in Evangelical proclamation we have expressed repentance in one key only – in the moral key, where it is all too easy for repentance to mean only guilt. True repentance occurs whenever and wherever we are led to exclaim, 'God, now I see' – that moment of cosmic disclosure, as Ian Ramsey used to say; or as I would prefer to say, whenever and wherever 'the penny drops'. Of course, this can and should occur frequently, and perhaps primarily, in the moral field, but not exclusively. If beauty, truth and goodness belong together, then saints, artists, apologists, as well as preachers, will have a part to play in evoking this repentance in the proper sense, to the extent that all alike are captured by the same vision. Repentance is then seen more as a change of attitude and outlook, whereby we do not come to see a different world so much as the same old world very differently.

Surely there is a constant running through all this, namely, 'Sirs, we would see Jesus.' That, I believe, is still the unspoken cry of many 'outsiders' or 'gentiles' – or, as it is more forcefully represented in the NEB translation, 'Sirs, it's Jesus we want to see.' Sadly, the institutional Church is not the most transparent of icons to display Jesus either by its celebration or by its proclamation. As Richard Harries says in his book, *Art and the Beauty of God*, 'The greatest obstacle to the Christian truth is the Church, the Body of Christ, those of us who call ourselves believers but who nevertheless obscure rather than reveal his glory.'

For the Catholic evangelist, apologetics is necessarily all of a piece with beauty, truth and goodness. Since that is so, while in no way wishing to promote a mindless Christianity, we shall nevertheless not wish to restrict our presentation of the Gospel merely to words or simply to the cerebral functions. We live in an age when the right-hand side of the brain is reasserting itself after some time of neglect, and while believing that there is still a sturdy ongoing work to do in the realm of apologetics – making sure that the Christian case does not go by default – I suspect that most people today are kept from faith for other reasons than merely reasons of the reason.

For Hans Urs von Balthasar beauty, or more exactly its manifestation in the beauty-glory of Christ, is the neglected aspect of Catholic faith, life and thinking. For von Balthasar, the God who dramatically pours out his goodness on the cross and in the blood of his Son, draws humankind into the truth and 'the logic of the cross' by the leading of the Holy Spirit. Von Balthasar's theology provides a map which draws together the aesthetic, the drama and the logic of the Christian faith in ways which can enrich a multi-dimensional presentation of the Christian reality, using media that speak more eloquently to our age than the narrow Christian apologetics we practised in the recent past.

Bernard Levin writes: 'The artist – the real artist – is not painting a milk jug, or sunflowers, or the Crucifixion. He is painting the truth.'[2] Later in the same book he goes on to assert that the ultimate wonder of all Shakespeare's work is that it is true. The same with music. Levin continues by asserting that the great composers and writers are intent upon saying to us in different languages, modes and styles: 'Look! This is the nature of things, this contradictory inter-play of light and shadow, agitation and stillness, height and depth, suspense and fulfilment, gravity and laughter, question and answer, conflict and resolution, chaos and order. This is how things are; yet within them and beyond them there is ultimate meaning and transcendent beauty which, once glimpsed, changes everything.'[3]

Put another way, if Christianity is true it is true because it is true and not because it is Christianity.

A EUCHARISTIC AND PRIESTLY SPIRITUALITY
The third essential ingredient in any Catholic evangelism is spirituality. Rightly perceived it will bind everything else

into a single whole, expressed through the daily lifestyle of the people of God. The Catholic witness in Anglicanism over the past 150 years has been unbelievably successful in establishing the Eucharist as the central and distinctive act of worship of God's people. But that is only half the battle. The other half is to live in accordance with it. It is precisely because the fourth evangelist presents eucharistic living from the very outset of his gospel that he feels free to give no one specific place for the actual institution of the Eucharist in the chronology of his gospel record. In John we see a Christ who handles the whole of life euchar- istically, for whom the whole of life is a sacrament and a sign, so that the part consecrates the whole.

Until we can begin to see as baptised Christians our identity as embodying the object of our adoration – eating the Body to become the Body – and at that, a Body which must be continually broken in order that it may be given for the life of the world, the Church will always be that most terrible of distortions, namely a self-serving ghetto, recruiting for membership. Those words attributed to Augustine come to mind: 'You are the body of Christ. That is to say, you must be taken, blessed, broken and given, in order that you may become vehicles of the eternal charity.' We shall never have that unique relationship to the rest of the world unless we see our story, our identity and our purpose as intimately related to the vocation of the cruci- fied, risen and outpouring Christ. Rather, we shall be in serious danger of becoming a high-church variety of the worst kind of mega-church evangelists. We are not in busi- ness to run the world or to be another large corporation taking the world over in the name of the Kingdom. In the words of the early second-century letter to Diognetus, 'what the soul is to the body, so is the Church to the world'. That is our calling.

Our attitude to the prevailing culture of the day must have about it this fourfold, redemptive and divinising activity of the Eucharist. 'He took: he blessed, he broke, he gave.' 'What he did not take, he did not redeem,' claims one of the Fathers. There is no such thing as an inculturated gospel. The Church must pour itself into, empty itself out into the world. It must embrace the flesh of the world and

19

– more than that – it must give thanks to God and, in so doing, as in the Old Testament, we shall *bless* the world. Until we have loved the world that much and God that much in His created order – *in* all things, as well as *above* all things – we cannot hope to enter fully into the struggle of working together with God in the reordering of this world until it becomes the Kingdom of our Christ and of His God. And we do this precisely because God is always *in* it all, as well as *beyond* it all; in it, by reason of the creation and the incarnation; beyond it, because of the ascension and the taking back of our humanity into the Godhead. Only such a fully sacramental, incarnational and indeed trinitarian theology of creation will provide such a vision for the enriching as well as for the transformation of all cultures.

So, if the Eucharist is not so much a service, but more a way of life – indeed, a way of seeing the divinisation of the whole life – so intercession is not so much a way of praying, but more a way of living: the new way of living, a distinctively vicarious way of living for others. William Temple was right: 'The Church is the only society which exists for the sake of those who are not members of it.'

Like Aaron of old, God's people come before God daily wearing the ephod of Christ, and daily plead the cause of all those in need of any kind, and especially of those who do not know the Lord Jesus. If we are truly to be the priestly people of God – that priesthood of all believers, which is not the same as the priesthood of every believer – then, partaking in the priesthood of the one true High Priest, we also will ever live to make intercession, not only in our prayers but in our lives. This will affect our worship at every point. 'At all times and in all places and in all styles' will be the principle which determines our services. Cell, congregation and cathedral will represent a diversity of worship styles, but we need to be mindful always that although worship can be informal, it must never be trivial. Music, drama, poetry, colour, lights, incense, silence, symbol as well as words – all alike will help to wing us to heaven and to lift up our heavy hearts in intercession, adoration and praise.

For it is wonder, and its place in our lives, which needs to be reclaimed for an age which has been rendered almost catatonic by the explosion of the information media. Surely to be 'lost in wonder, love and praise' is what we are all reaching for intuitively – and not least the young. We seek transcendence. There are many at the moment who through drugs and erotomania are seeking to climb up some other way. They are strongly in reaction against the reductionism of a post-Cartesian society: 'I am what I earn; I am what I think; I shop therefore I am (Tesco ergo sum – to quote Robert Warren); I am what I do; I am my sexuality; I am what I own.' In the face of this, Catholic Christians will refuse to settle for anything less than: 'I worship, therefore I am.' In the words of the psychiatrist in Peter Shaeffer's play *Equus*: 'If you don't worship, you'll shrink, it's as brutal as that.' It is against such reductionism and 'shrinkage' of the human race that Catholic evangelism must seek to pit itself at every turn. We have the food to satisfy the hunger for transcendence, the hunger for worship, in our hands.

The Practice of Catholic Evangelism

Ultimately, the proof of any Catholic evangelistic pudding will as always be found in the eating. Are we prepared to get stuck in and to do it, rather than merely to attend conferences to talk about it, or even worse to pore over our computers to write books about it? The famous saying of G.K. Chesterton comes to our rescue in our pathetic failings in such evangelistic endeavours: 'If a job's worth doing, it's worth doing *badly*!' What ultimately cuts the ice is disarmingly simple: a twofold passion – a passion for souls, wedded to a passion for the Kingdom. The world and the Church are on a sliding scale somewhere variably between the two. Surely there must be a necessary 'provisionality' about the Church. We have almost, if I dare say it, 'to care and not to care' about ecclesiastical structures, ministry and domestic life. We must sit lightly to what it is to be 'Church' and we must never, as Michael Ramsey used to remind us, take ourselves as 'Church' too seriously – while always seeking to take a passion for God's Kingdom and for souls very seriously indeed.

At the conclusion of a characteristically remarkable

21

sermon by Bishop John Taylor, he said: ' "Father, your reign, your Kingdom come, your will be done on earth, as it is in heaven. Give us today our . . ." What?' There is good evidence, John Taylor claims, that the word Jesus used next means, not 'daily' but 'of the coming day'.[4] So it might be better rendered – ' "Give us tomorrow's bread today" – like the man in the parable who was shameless enough to pester his neighbour in the middle of the night for a loaf of bread instead of waiting for the morning. Give us tomorrow's bread, the bread of Kingdom Come, today. They are words not so much of petition as of commitment: "We'll live God's tomorrow now." ' And by God, and with His grace, as Catholic evangelists we dare not settle for anything less!

In conclusion, here are five sound-bites concerning the practice of what I have been outlining and hopefully envisioning. What might all this look like in action in rural and urban parishes up and down the country?

Presence We must understand ourselves as the real presence of Jesus locally in His Body, doing and saying what Jesus did and said when he came into Galilee heralding the Kingdom. For the promise is to us in this generation as at the first: 'The things that I do you will do, and greater things, because I go to the Father.' Empowered by the gifts of the Spirit of the risen Christ, we are God's people locally witnessing to resurrection in our everyday lives, and therefore necessarily an apostolic people. For the Church only becomes truly apostolic when it can witness to resurrection and to a God who is up to His eyes in the midst of it all – in the mess of it all and therefore in the mystery of it all.

Prayer The Body of Christ in each place is a cell of prayer, again rooted locally, living and praying for the wider community, intent upon discovering the needs, concerns, hopes and fears of the community. The local church constitutes what might be termed (again to quote Robert Warren) 'A Local Neighbourhood Watch Committee'. We are 'God's spies' in that and in every sense.

Evangelism as a process rather than a crisis We need to nurture a kind of evangelism in which maintenance is not contrasted with mission, but in which mission is seen rather as doing maintenance in a missionary way. We must resist the temptation to join up congregations and centralise. Centralise and you will shrink: decentralise and you could grow. A Church – like a nation – cannot serve both God and market forces!

From our pitch to theirs We go out to others, but not with a view to drawing them ultimately on to our pitch: real life blossoms where it takes root. Belonging, believing and behaving are better coming in that order, rather than in the reverse order which traditional evangelism has tended to follow. We must present Christianity as Someone to follow, rather than as something to swallow!

Pilgrimage and provisionality We have to be the Church on the move in every sense, as a model for growth, change and flexibility. 'To live is to change and to be perfect is to have changed often,' said Newman, with his understanding of organic development and evolving life. If faith and order belong together in the Catholic understanding, then the structures of our Church need to resemble more those of a tent, rather than those of a large concrete building. Provisionality can only be your watchword if you envisage yourselves as a Church on the move. Unprotected and vulnerable, offering a poverty of spirit (God's street people and nomadic spiritual gypsies) and so demonstrating a solidarity with the powerless – only such a vulnerable community of faith will render the Church credible as salt, light and leaven for the rest of the world. Now that the Labour party appears to be set on abandoning the poor for the middle-class lobby, it could well be that only the Church will be left to be identified with the powerless. After all, that was once the proud claim of Catholic evangelists, in the days when Anglo-Catholics were conspicuous for their work in the cities and urban priority areas of the Industrial Revolution.

Over the vesting chest in the sacristy at St Matthew's

23

Westminster, where I am presently an episcopal squatter of sorts, are the words that embody for me the flesh and blood of what we might well call a hands-on, Catholic evangelism.

> You are Christians.
> Then your Lord is one and the same
> with Jesus on the throne of his glory
> with Jesus in his blessed sacrament
> with Jesus received into your hearts in communion
> with Jesus who is mystically with you as you pray
> and with Jesus enshrined in the hearts and bodies
> of his brothers and sisters up and down the world.
>
> Now go out into the highways and hedges
> and look for Jesus in the ragged and naked
> in the oppressed and sweated
> in those who have lost hope
> and in those who are struggling to make good.
>
> Look for Jesus in them; and when you find him
> gird yourselves with his towel of fellowship
> and wash his feet in the person of his brethren.

In affirming Catholicism, or better still in affirming Catholic Evangelism, may nothing less than such a vision be our story and our song, as a pilgrim Church on the move. As St Augustine exhorts us in one of his finest sermons: 'Sing Alleluia and keep on walking.'

Notes

1 L. Newbigin, *The Gospel in a Pluralist Society*, p. 227.
2 Bernard Levin, *Enthusiasms* (Jonathan Cape, 1983), pp. 72–3.
3 ibid.
4 These observations are taken from a sermon by Bishop John V. Taylor at the opening of the Bath Festival at Bath Abbey, 21 May 1995.

2 Evangelism and Worship*

David Stancliffe

From where does the Church derive its power to convert? It was the Church's worship which converted me to the truth of the gospel, the beauty of God and the possibility – I hesitate to say 'reality' – of the Kingdom. If the Church is sign, instrument and foretaste of the Kingdom, worship is where those abstractions are – or ought to be – made concrete. We ought to be able to say with confidence, 'Share with us in the breaking of the bread, and you will see Christ crucified among his people, forming them as his Body; and this feast will give you a glimpse of heaven.' For it is in worship that what the Church believes and does is earthed and made visible. Worship, and the eucharistic worship which is at the centre of Catholic life and practice, offers us a pattern where welcome and belonging leads to a deepening relationship with Christ and forms us as a people on the way, so that people can get from that process the confidence to be themselves, and also the vision of where God would have them be. While this process may be properly 'affirming', what concerns me most is that it should be genuinely 'Catholic'.

No account of Catholic evangelism, therefore, can be complete without a comment on the power of worship, whether for good or ill. And I say 'for good or ill' because I am aware that worship – whether it is a funeral at which the whole village is present, or a jolly Rite A parish communion screaming against a Tractarian church in a suburb of London, or a clan baptism with 100 in the family party inserted into the sung mass of an inner-urban parish where there are 35 regular communicants (all over 60) because it

*© David Stancliffe 1996

25

is the liturgically proper thing to do, or the consecration of a bishop where the ceremonial of 1662 has been imported unaltered into the ASB rite, or an 8 a.m. communion service celebrated by someone who does not understand what Cranmer was trying to do, or the testimony, baptism, confirmation and first communion of a teenager in front of her sceptical as well as her believing friends – worship can have the power to convert or (and alas, this is more frequent) to repel. It is not just that the conduct of worship can be amazingly incompetent; it is that people have a very real sense of whether what is being offered is the genuine article or not.

In this chapter, therefore, I am seeking to discern where the reality, the genuine article lies. I do it in the context of this movement we call Affirming Catholicism because I am clear that a crucial contribution of the Catholic tradition is to continue to bridge the apparent gap between Christ's presence in the Eucharist and his presence in the troubled and broken lives of his people: two real presences which are too often felt in fact as real absences.

Let me start obliquely. In an article in *The Tablet* on what was happening to the Christian faith in Germany, this statement leapt out at me: 'Between 1945 and 1968 both the Catholic and the Protestant Churches in Germany were in an extraordinarily favourable position. The proportion of those going to church was at its peak – 55 per cent of Catholics in 1963 and 15 per cent of Protestants.' The article then charts the decline in both traditions. But the contrast of the two percentages is not the main point or purpose of the article, nor is the extraordinary difference between them commented on. Indeed, it is simply one of our regular assumptions now as much as 30 years ago that Catholics go to church and Protestants do not.

Why, I wondered, should this be? While I realise that there are a number of factors to be taken into account, one distinction seems obvious: Catholics believe that something happens in church, Protestants do not. While the Catholic tradition rejoices in the living presence of Christ among his people, focused in the eucharistic action which not only expresses but creates the Church as the Body of Christ, the Protestant tradition remembers with thankfulness the time when he was on earth, and hopes people will be inspired to be good. From my experience, the one question which Roman Catholic priests quite rightly raise, when on holiday you ask if you may receive the Sacrament at their mass, is, 'Do you believe that Christ is really present in the Sacrament?' But present how and where? In the elements? Or in those who after giving thanks and breaking the bread receive them? Or in the minds of those who remember with thanksgiving? Or in the eucharistic community as it is renewed and made one? When the Roman Catholics held a congress of lay people in Liverpool in the early 1980s they came out with the slogan, 'We are the Easter people and our song is Alleluia.' Were we ever able to mount such a venture (imagine the Church of England being able to mount anything like that; it would require years of committee meetings to get it near the tip of anyone's agenda) I am tempted to think that our slogan might be, 'We are the Christmas people and our song is Once in Royal David's City.' We suffer from a terribly uncreative, nostalgic longing for the past that is romantic, not Catholic. We look back, I take it, in order to understand where we are in the present so that we can move forward in confidence, knowing that we are doing it according to the mind of Christ, and that we are not making it up as we go along. But our concentration on the retrospective means we risk losing the actual, the here-and-now miracle, which is the key Catholic perception.

These caricatures are limited and unfair, but they serve to underline a fundamental difference about how Christ's presence with his people is understood. One tradition emphasises the Living Word and locates it in the pages of Holy Scripture, from which the hermeneutic skills and the power of the preacher can draw out a story that lives in the present, and which song anchors in human hearts and experience. Our tradition celebrates the coming of that Word made flesh in our midst as a continuous present, charging human experience with the pre-echo of glory. This presence is focused in, though not confined to, the sacramental acts of Christ in his Church; and those who celebrate the sacraments renew their encounter with the living Christ, and learn to recognise, celebrate and partici-

27

pate in the divine activity, frequently masked though it is by natural disorder and human wrongdoing in the present world.

Or is this merely wishful thinking? Is there in fact no connection between the world of faith and the world as most people know and experience it? I believe that it is vitally important for the health and vitality of the whole Church that we rediscover – or rather reinterpret – the essential relationship between God and the world, if the practice of the Christian faith (and of Christian worship in particular) is not increasingly to be seen as a dreamworld exercise. What we do in church – the sacraments that we celebrate and the story we tell – is, we believe, the key to the truth about who we are and the purpose of human life. What is more, our celebration of this story and these sacraments is claimed to be a channel of God's grace: it changes reality objectively as well as changing us. If that activity is grounded in no more than fond memory and wishful make-believe, then we have nothing to offer and, as St Paul said, 'We are of all men most to be pitied.'

To many on the fringes of the Church, who like to know that worship continues and to eavesdrop on it from time to time, who recognise that churches are 'a serious place on serious earth', and that when they enter them they are standing 'where prayer is wont to be valid', worship tends to be just this kind of fond memory, reminding them of a world which they would dearly love to own, but believe to have vanished for ever. They ache for the old rites, but when they hear them they seem to have lost their magic. It is perhaps a peculiar legacy of the characteristic mix of English scepticism and Anglican mistrust of enthusiasm. People will go to a Shakespeare play like *Hamlet* and feel (for all that it is 'only a play') that they have been changed, and put in touch with a deeper reality. Shakespeare answers real questions. To them we have to demonstrate that worship, and the celebration of the sacraments in particular, is not mere play-acting, but the channel by which we enter into the reality which is God, as he enters into us.

Then there are others for whom the whole legacy of rite and sacrament, of resonant texts and allusive phrases, is meaningless mumbo-jumbo. They long to be embraced by the divine love, and sometimes mistake the warmth of human love for the divine. Liturgically, the exchange of the Peace is their high-point, and they will chose a place of worship – they may well be in a house-church or an independent church of like-minded spirits rather than in their parish church – more for its music style than for anything else. They live in a culture of decency and self-improvement, and we fail them equally. To them, too, we have to demonstrate that worship, and the celebration of the sacraments in particular, is not a barrier to communion with the living God but a means of his grace and sign of his real presence.

What do we have to offer? One possible approach is that of Roger Grainger, who has written extensively in the area of religious phenomenology, and most recently in a small book entitled *The Ritual Image*. He started his career as a Shakespearean actor and spent most of his working life as chaplain of a psychiatric hospital. Commenting on John 1:14, 'The Word was made flesh and dwelt among us', he writes:

> For Christians, theology and anthropology are identified. Our task is to rediscover the life of theology through our own lives, and the warfare – not only spiritual, but neccessarily political – in which we are involved. When we look back over the ages, we can identify times of social and cultural conflict as periods of intense spiritual activity. The links between history and theology are forged in the white heat of circumstance; they do not emerge as a result of an academic exercise aimed at achieving some intellectual synthesis. We re-discover ourselves by re-claiming our story, the things that have happened to us, the experience of love and rejection, estrangement and reconciliation, crisis and deliverance, that have left their imprint on our lives. We make our story part of ourselves; it is our life, our identity.
>
> How do we do this? The answer is obvious. We do it by ritual, the artistic re-creation of emotional truth in terms of spiritual significance. Because its truth is emotional and spiritual, ritual is more concerned with the evocation of meanings than the literal reproduction of historical circumstances. It is symbolic, rather than literal. It has the power to affect conclusions we

29

draw from events in the light of a significance which transcends history and alters our attitude towards ourselves and other people. In the polarizing presence of the rite the fact is brought home that we do not simply have a story, we are one, each of us. To become a self is to appropriate a story, for the primary datum of human experience is story and story, the intermeshing of the ways that things have happened to us. On this our knowledge of ourselves and of one another depends. Also our knowledge of God.

We believe that God has made our story his own. Narrative theology forms the third partner in the movements towards re-rooting theology in actual personal experience. The meaning of personal life is experienced in story form. If you ask me to tell you about myself, we end up exchanging stories. The form taken by our experience of enslavement and liberation is the story of our suffering and deliverance. What we offer to God is our story – ours and his.[1]

Roger Grainger is serious about the quest for reality, and locates it in our story, which, as he says, God has made his own. For him, ritual is 'the timeless location for the identification of the human with the divine, just as human life is experienced historically as narrative, in the ritual format divinity is itself given a story, so that our human stories may be touched and changed by contact with the focused imagery of the divine. Stories do not necessarily have words.'[2] With this analysis in our minds and his plea for a renewed appreciation of ritual, let us look at what is really happening in worship and see if we can detect where its power to convert lies.

Let me offer you two vignettes: the first is an account by Lara, a young Quaker, aged 11, who recalls her first impressions at a Russian Christmas vigil.

> We [a group of about 15] arrived in the dark to see ladies in fur coats going into a large stone church. It had originally belonged to the Church of England but had been sold to the Russian Orthodox Church. In order to buy it, the priest had told the people they would have to sacrifice everything they had. One elderly lady donated her gold teeth, which had fallen out.
>
> We were greeted by the head priest when we entered. He explained Russian Orthodox worship by saying it was similar

to Quakerism (it seemed very different to me): the congregation stood in silence, unless you were too old to stand. They believe a person can only reach the inner part of their spiritual self like this. Unlike Quakerism, there was a lot of bowing and crossing during the two-hour-long service.

After the priest was finished speaking, we went to buy candles. The church was lit by hundreds and hundreds of them. It was amazing. There was a ceremony before putting each candle in its holder. First, you walked up the aisle and kissed the icon nearest where you wished to place your candle. Then you melted the underside of the candle to make it fit the holder.

The church was impressive. At the top of the main aisle there was a screen painted with saints. The area within the screen was the 'sanctuary' where only the priests could go. It was an inner place of worship where I saw the priest's robes being blessed before they were put on.

Music was an important part of the worship. The choir began the service by singing in Russian. The singing was beautiful and rich. A chanted reading in Russian followed, singing followed that.

A priest from behind the sanctuary flung open the golden gates to reveal himself. He was an older man with a grey beard. He wore a black tall hat which had black fabric flowing to the floor. His deep crimson robe was trimmed with gold and underneath he wore a white and gold robe. He turned and crossed himself. The congregation did the same.

Several times during the service a long line of priests walked down the main aisle swinging incense. They wore elaborate gold robes and wore jewelled crowns. The priests went on to a stage and blessed oil, wine and bread. People from the congregation had crosses painted on their heads with this oil. Two bibles were read from during the service, one with a silver cover inlaid with jewels, the other with a gold cover inlaid with jewels.

As I was leaving this amazing service I passed by an open coffin with a body in it. A member of the congregation had died that morning and it was the custom to place the body in the church.

This Russian Orthodox service was stunning. I feel privileged and honoured to have been able to attend.[3]

Notice what works for Lara: the welcome, the richness,

the movement of those who light the myriad candles, or who swing the incense; the fact that the congregation had crosses painted on the foreheads with oil and that the bibles were important enough to be jewelled – no reading out of 'missalettes' there – and not one word about what was read. She was swept up into the movement, a movement from darkness to light, from death to life, and the open coffin as she leaves – with a member of the congregation who has gone one step further in the company of the saints along the road to heaven – seems a natural part of the experience. Without understanding what was happening, she was content – 'privileged and honoured', she says – to have been included. There was a strong sense of belonging and communion, of a thread linking this world and the next.

The other vignette is more artful. It comes from a different century, from *A Sentimental Journey* by Laurence Sterne, and is called 'The Grace'.

> When supper was over, the old man gave a knock upon the table with the haft of his knife, to bid them prepare for the dance. The moment the signal was given, the women and girls ran all together into a back appartment to tie up their hair and the young men to the door to wash their faces and to change their sabots; and in three minutes every soul was ready upon a little esplanade before the house to begin. The old man and his wife came out last, and placing me betwixt them, sat down upon a sofa of turf by the door.
>
> The old man had some fifty years ago been no mean performer on the vielle, and, at the age he was then of, touch'd it well enough for the purpose. His wife sung now-and-then a little to the tune, then intermitted, and join'd her old man again as their children and grand-children danced before them.
>
> It was not until the middle of the second dance, when from some pauses in the movement wherein they all seemed to look up, I fancied I could distinguish an elevation of spirit different from that which is the cause or the effect of simple jollity. In a word, I thought I beheld *Religion* mixing in the dance – but as I had never seen her so engaged, I should have look'd upon it now as one of the illusions of an imagination which is eternally misleading me, had not the old man, as soon as the dance ended,

said that this was their constant way; and that all his life long he had made it a rule, after supper was over, to call out his family to dance and rejoice; believing, he said, that a cheerful and contented mind was the best sort of thanks to Heaven an illiterate peasant could pay.

'Or a learned prelate either,' said I.

Again, the dance – that image of inclusion and energy – captures the sense of movement, where new dancers and so new life is woven into the continuing tradition of the family. Communion with the deity is not a moment to be achieved so much as a life to be expressed, enjoyed and shared. In worship that is worth the name – and you will have your own experiences to set alongside my vignettes – we can detect the experience of change, of transformation as well as that of communion. True worship mirrors the divine activity: the Son shares the Father's life with us, that we might offer ourselves in him to the Father. The central point in this interchange, where the human and divine are seen to be perfectly one, is the cross – that moment of death which seems to be the gateway to life, like the grain of wheat which, unless it falls on the earth and dies, remains alone; but if it dies, it bears a rich harvest. And that moment – is it a death or a birth? – is echoed in the rites. What happens in that moment when the unregenerate infant is plunged beneath the waters and rises to new life? What makes a motley assembly of human beings into the Body of Christ? Where is the Body of Christ? Is it located in the consecrated bread on the altar or in the community which celebrates? Or both? Our attempts to be precise about these questions tend to focus on the wrong thing: it is easier to focus on objects rather than processes, and try to fix what is essentially developing in the equivalent of aspic. No photograph of a butterfly in flight, however perfect, can capture the essential quality of its flitting movement.

I want to emphasise the importance of this difference between objects and processes, and to stress that the processes are as real and as important as the objects. Indeed, they may be more so, because the processes are focused on what is happening, what is changing, and alert us to mistrust what seems too static. Turn the developing process of

33

the way in which two people relate to one another, for example, into a substantive like 'marriage', and we run the risk of fossilising the relationship by thinking of it in more static terms than we should. Relationships are living things and always changing: they may grow or they may wither and even die. The tendency of Latin-based languages to use abstract nouns for processes (especially when this is done by the tidy-minded for the purpose of legal definition) has not helped our understanding of the marriage relationship, or of how to celebrate it. We put all our eggs in the basket of 'the wedding'. Nor has it been helpful in understanding that delicate chemistry of change and transformation which is the basis of our eucharistic theology, and indeed of our whole relationship with God. Making eucharist, becoming Church, becoming Christlike, is to enter a dynamic process of movement into God, in response to the gift he shares with us, of which the Christian community or fellowship is a visible sign.

So what processes like this are at work in worship to make communion happen? The answer to this must be, 'the same as are at work in any relationship, where rigidity is the kiss of death'. This has led some people to imagine that the only true communion in worship is spontaneous, unstructured and free. Far from it. The structure of the liturgy holds together the partners in the relationship – ourselves and God – in the way that the court and rules make possible a game of tennis, or language and syntax make possible a conversation: without these, there is only the random hitting of balls around or a series of grunts and shouts which never allow minds to meet, still less a conversation to develop. For a relationship with God to develop, and for the process of change to take place, we need the grammar and syntax of words and music, and the courts and rules of sacred space and the liturgical year. So let us take an example, and consider space and syntax first.

For a long time I have been struck by the way Thomas Cranmer used the medieval churches his brave new world had inherited from the medieval Church in England. Think of them in your mind's eye, or picture a neo-medieval creation like South Creake or Blisland. In the nave there are benches around the wall, and here the congregation gathers. Divided from them by a screen is the chancel, where the priest offers the mass at a distant altar. Like the temple of old, there is a space for us and a space for God. The two – the holy God and the common people – are kept apart by the screen, and over it, set against the background of the doom painting, stands the rood – Christ on the cross with St Mary and St John at his feet. Only that death, only that one, perfect sacrifice, can rend the curtain and open the way for his erring people to full communion with God. Only by that one sacrifice on Calvary, re-presented in each eucharistic celebration, are man and God, heaven and earth, the human and the divine, made one.

Cranmer, clear about the centrality of the cross, took this ancient division of the screen, this historical divide, and – unlike the continental reformers who, for the most part, disregarded the chancels and created a church-in-the-round in the nave – reused the series of spaces, but functionally rather than theologically. His pastoral rites – funerals and marriages – begin at the porch or the door. In the nave the Word is preached, and so that its edifying effects could be appreciated, the nave is pewed like a synagogue or schoolroom. To that company an invitation is issued, and then those who wish to 'draw near with faith' come to kneel around the Holy Table to make their confession and – in Cranmer's particularly dramatic way, woven into the middle of his eucharistic prayer – receive the Sacrament. It is not my intention to examine the development of Cranmer's eucharistic theology, but simply to note that in his order for Holy Communion that magic barrier of the rood screen is pierced: the communicants step through that physical gateway which symbolises the *limen* or threshold between the human and the divine. Cranmer grasps that, in Christ, man and God are one, and that an intelligent celebration of the sacraments demands a physical transference or movement between one space and the other. The Word is proclaimed and preached, and God's people respond with the offering of themselves, their souls and bodies. Receiving the body and blood of Christ, they are assured that they are 'very members incorporate in the mystical Body ... which is the blessed company of all faithful people'. The genius of Cranmer's liturgy, however idiosyncratic it may be, is that it takes this sense of movement and growth seriously.

Modern liturgical fashion scores less well, interestingly: the demand for visibility has tended to turn the congregation from being participants into spectators. Today's most favoured liturgical arrangements in modern churches – a kind of apron stage with all the liturgical objects (font, ambo, presidential chair, tabernacle, altar, lectern) arranged on the performance area – does nothing to develop the tradition of transformation. In fact, it seems rather to reinforce the Victorian view that going to church was a matter of sitting, listening, assenting and departing to put the duties you had been taught into practice. Such an arrangement turns the liturgical action of the whole assembly into a spectacle conducted by specialised performers, and reduces the role of the congregation to passive onlookers instead of the principal persons in the drama. In their most extreme form, such as the completely circular cathedral of Christ the King in Liverpool, the buildings are entirely static and inward-looking, reflecting an ecclesiology which is dominated by the idea of the Church as the Body of Christ, a model which can be cloyingly claustrophobic and cliquishly self-centred, as the Church has found to its cost over the past 25 years or so.

I had not realised this with such clarity until I went to a number of monastic houses – St Benoît-sur-Loire, Ewell Monastery in Kent, and the mixed community at Imshausen, for example – where the eucharistic liturgy is celebrated either in a series of rooms or in different spaces within the same large church. In these communities each space has a focus, yet each liturgical encounter takes you a stage further in the developing relationship with God and pushes you forward to the next space, with its different focus, and so creates a more dynamic celebration.

How are we to image the liturgy so that it can have both an engagement with the community which celebrates and also a sense of transformation and direction; so that both the immanence of God (the sense of his coming among us and being discovered to be active in our midst) and his transcendence (the sense that he is far greater than ever we could conceive and is calling us out of our present darkness into his marvellous light) are held together? Worship must be earthed before it transforms; and as St Athanasius said of the incarnation, 'what God did not assume, he did not redeem'. These two poles are essential. Catholic Christians will see them earthed in the twin peaks of the liturgical year: the celebration of the incarnation in the cycle centred on Christmas, and the feast of our redemption, centred on Easter. These two major cycles celebrate aspects of God's relationship with us which are not exclusive but complementary. But Catholic Christians may not so readily acknowledge that these twin peaks must also be earthed in the daily experience of people. Reality and redemption, acknowledging that in the ordinariness of daily domestic life are the glints of gold, whether we are talking of relationships, work (however uncreative), or just (or should I say supremely?) the business of trying to be yourself. These are the places where the Church has a duty to uncover reality and redemption, and to help people be aware of the movement that is already going on in their lives, the seeds of change and development, even if not of obvious hope. This is a crucial task for the Church to be undertaking, whether on the parochial or national level, yet many clergy feel unconfident in helping to discern these processes. You can tell it from their sermons. You cannot preach convincingly unless you have this direct relationship with your parish, which is one of the things bishops find most difficult. (Lay people please help, and remind us that we are still part of the laity too.)

The best of our liturgical celebrations, like the best of our church buildings and all of the Church's sacraments, will be earthed, bedded into actuality. They will offer us a starting-point 'where we are', as they say. But they will not leave us there: having engaged with us, they will take us beyond where we could have conceived of getting on our own. This is the power and the promise of God's transforming love. And, very simply, it is the model of how God comes among us, shares our human life, and so redeems and transforms us in the birth, baptism, ministry, passion and resurrection of Jesus Christ. Without the incarnation there could be no redemption; yet incarnation on its own (though it might have given us a friend and companion in our distress) could not have transformed our lot. If the sacraments are celebrations of transformation, snapshots of a process, they derive their power from the human experience of the basic realities on which they are based – bread and wine, the food of men and angels; water with its possibilities of death and a new birth into light; oil for healing and suppleness as well as for king-making; the embrace of reconciliation and the joining of hands in marriage. These touch deep chords in human experience; and yet each contains the promise of growth, renewal and transformation.

Take the Eucharist, for example, and see how the pattern of engagement and development works out in practice. To begin with, there is a liturgy of preparation and approach – what the Canadian Book of Alternative Services calls 'The Gathering of the Community'. This is essentially a rite of preparation, a rite with an Advent feel, looking towards the coming of God among his people and taking seriously the prophetic injunction to prepare and turn to God. This liturgy may take place before the doors of the church in the courtyard, or in the vestibule; it may take place the night before or the morning after; but its function is the same – to weld into one, to focus on God's agenda and not ours in such a way as to allow people to move forward into worship as one body, expecting that God will come among them and speak to them in word and sacrament.

Then there is what we have come to know as 'The Ministry of the Word'. At the heart of this is not a didactic exposition of Scripture – the kind of thing that is more suited to a lecture theatre or schoolroom – but a vivid encounter with the Word made flesh. In the medieval church, one of the rare sallies west of the rood screen was for the reading of the gospel – a sally in the sense that God in Christ had entered his world, to be known and recognised as he transformed darkness into light. It is not simply a matter of passing on information about God: it is an encounter with the Living God himself who has abandoned his kingly throne and pitched his tent in our midst. This is why the eucharistic lectionary has such a different character from the lectionary of the Daily Office, where regular rumination on Scripture in sequence allows us to absorb the tradition so that it becomes part of the way we live and reflect. In the Eucharist, we expect to meet the living Christ as he comes among us. The point of his coming is not to give information, but to disclose God's glory. Nor is the glory all imported. Some of it is there already, though hidden and masked by the layers of dirt. In Irenaeus's thinking, though man is created in God's image, that image indicates only potential, a potential that needs to be transformed into likeness: 'For the glory of God is a man fully alive; and the life of man is the vision of God.' At the heart of the Ministry of the Word is this patterning of the imprint of the divine life, as it is made visible and concrete in the Word made flesh, in Jesus Christ. It is offered as a paradigm against which we measure our aspirations and achievements, and the Ministry of the Word moves naturally through proclamation and exposition to intercession. It is at this moment that our longings for transformation become focused and actualised in particular human stories of particular peoples and situations and individuals, where we long to see the divine work of reconciliation and re-creation take root and blossom. That is the point where we ally ourselves with Christ 'who ever lives to make intercession for us', praying that his one prayer to the Father – Your will be done, not mine – may also be ours. This is the moment when the focus shifts from what God is doing among us and what he may be going to do among us – the realisation of God's eternal purposes in the space and time of human existence – to what God is eternally doing and has ultimately accomplished for us in the life, death and resurrection of Christ.

It is at this point that we make a movement from the temporal to the eternal, from our life to his, from receiving to offering, from reflection to realisation. As we come to surround the table which is both the focus of our common life and the sign in our midst of the promise of the banquet in the eternal Kingdom, we model that Kingdom on earth – or rather, we are modelled by Christ's passion and resurrection to represent it, however imperfectly. The icon of perfect love, the image of the Holy Trinity, is not some

39

abstract conceptual diagram, using a physical analogy to represent the interrelationship of the persons of the Trinity; that icon is the Church at the Eucharist, the human community gathered around the table of the Lord. By his death on the cross made real in our midst in the broken bread on the altar and in the palms of our hands, our broken and scattered lives are made whole as God brings life out of death, and discloses his power made perfect in our human weakness. This is the central mystery of the Christian life, that by the death of one person, life has been restored to all; and it is by the constant rehearsal of this passage from death to life in each celebration of the Eucharist that the Church is gradually formed and made Christlike. This is a crucial truth to uphold in an age when, for a variety of social, political and economic reasons, stress on the individual's worth, potential and achievements has led us to prize the individual's (and hence our own) security and significance above notions of the common good of all. Our culture, with its message of salvation and security through acquisition and personal defence – whether that is achieved by winning the Lottery or by taking out yet another insurance policy – prizes getting above giving, self-seeking above sacrifice. The Christian tradition stands for the absolute opposite: that true happiness is to be found only in losing yourself, and that the way to fulfilment in the steps of Christ is to give without counting the cost.

Do we actually believe this, this extraordinary reversal which is at the heart of the faith, and is the kernel of every eucharistic celebration? Do we expect to be changed by our weekly, daily participation in the Eucharist? And if we do, as we must, are we ready to live by it, and to put it into practice? This is not only a question for us as individuals. Does the Church model this sacrificial sense of communion? Does it transform us from being a scattered group of selfish human individuals into a divine community which *does* reflect an image of the Kingdom?

What the world needs more than anything else is a sign of transformation, a sign that the human community can live as one and transcend differences of gender, race, tribe, nation, wealth, colour and status. The Church will be genuinely evangelical, will be good news, only if this modelling is visible and apparent. And with all the clutter of our organisational life and our interminable debates and arguments it is difficult for this to seep through. But worship is the place where it can and must be visible. If we, at the heart of what we do as a Church community, cannot week by week and day by day model what the Kingdom is called to be, then we shall continue to be dismissed as irrelevant and hypocritical. For the most frequent charge levelled against the Church – quite justifiably – is that we do not practise what we preach.

So, finally, what should Catholic Anglicans practise as we attempt to live out our sacrificial calling? While it is tempting to set out a list of what we should be doing (like those lists of sins which used to be in the old manuals, and which you would never have thought of committing if you hadn't read them there), I must confine myself to some basic points.

First, may I remind you of the Benedictine order, which has had such a significant part to play in the formation of English Christianity. The Benedictine commitment is to *stabilitas* – which means not just stability in the sense of solidity, but something more like stickability. It means staying in the same place, always being there. In a highly mobile, swiftly changing culture, symbols of stability are crucial, and I do not believe that it is just curiosity that fills our cathedrals as they have never been filled before. Stability – always being there – evangelises. People need to know where to go to find God: they go to the Church and to the tradition. We have to keep these in good repair.

Second, hospitality. Hospitality is for me a richer and more dynamic concept than inclusivity. Benedictine hospitality urges us to receive guests as if they were Christ himself. People call us, call on us, for a huge variety of reasons. Attending to them is not only an exercise in hospitality, but an exercise in listening and learning. If we do not listen, there can be no conversation and no engagement, and we stop modelling the divine life which in the incarnation engages with our story in our terms.

Third, listening demands silence on our part. Let us have more attentive silence and resist the temptation to fill the Church's life with chatter, the ecclesial equivalent of wallpaper muzak. We have prophets, some of them in our company; let us listen to what they are saying.

Fourth, learning. Serious study, especially of the history of the Church, is a prerequisite if we are not to fall into the trap of blandness and cliché. I want to make a distinction between amassing information, and possibly drowning under it, so that we can't tell the wood from the trees, and discerning what is relevant. While it is important to discover who knows about what, and to use each other's skills, there is no substitute for clear thinking.

Fifth, there is the Christian social tradition. Where is it? It is all very well to model *koinonia* in the Eucharist, but have we now got sufficient energy to spare to put our faith into practice? This is what made the heroes of the past unstoppable and will make people take notice. Inevitably some time is spent in wondering how to attract people's notice to the rich Catholic inheritance of the Church, but we shall be judged by whether we succeed in defining and living out the essentials of the Catholic faith, or whether (as some people suspect) we are merely a band of adventurers, seeking a cause or two which may devour us.

So – establishing the essentials of the Catholic faith; exploring how best to live them; sharing them with those whom we welcome into our company by publications and persuasion; and remaining alert and joyful in the service of the risen Lord: that seems enough to be going on with. Let us practise what we preach.

Notes

1 R. Grainger, *The Ritual Image: A Phenomenology of Religious Experience* (Avon Books), pp. 4–5.

2 ibid., p. 6.

3 This account first appeared in *The Friend*, 3 February 1995, and is reprinted in *Sobernost*, vol. 17: 1.

3 The Church in Society*

John Habgood

I was intrigued last year to be introduced to a new concept in which I have some personal interest. It is the concept of Habgoodism, and it appeared in an article by Clifford Longley who identified it as, if not the cause, at least one of the underlying factors in the current British malaise. In brief, his argument was that there is a deep unreality at the heart of English culture, the theory of what he calls 'an Anglican state'. It is the belief that it is the duty of the Church of England to provide the 'public religion' of the English. And he concluded that since not all is well with English society, this must imply that something is seriously wrong with the religious and moral pillars which ought to be upholding it – pillars of which he sees myself as a chief defender. Hence Habgoodism.

In part, this is a familiar complaint. Clifford Longley has for years had an obsession with establishment, and I do not propose to rehearse familiar arguments about it. Nor do I want to comment on his drastic oversimplification of my views. But I am interested in the contrast he drew between the veterans who marched to celebrate VE-Day and for whom decent 'Anglican' values are still a reality and a token of what they fought for, and the under-40s who live in a different world. There are indeed serious questions about the kind of society we are now, and the kind of society we are likely to become. I quote from his article:

> England is a depressed nation, unsure of its own future, increasingly fractious. The English are among the most pessimistic in Europe. Facing the European Union, they sense how fragile their

*© John Habgood 1996

institutions are, how uncertain is the definition of Englishness and how vulnerable it seems, therefore, to foreign absorption. This is not the attitude of a self-confident people. A lot of this self-doubt is not primarily about Europe. It is a fear of change, fear of the different; fear, above all, of the future.

Is this true? Whether true or not, it seems to me a useful starting-point for an exploration of where we are as a Church and as a society in the context of a forward-looking faith, a faith which seeks to evangelise in both the Roman Catholic and the Evangelical senses of that word. I want to examine it from three perspectives: sociological, theological and European.

Sociological

For the sociology, I turn to Grace Davie's book *Religion in Britain since 1945* with the telling subtitle *Believing without Belonging*. The subtitle points to a phenomenon which is familiar to us all: not, as was once predicted, a wholesale shift to a secular society, but a persistence of interest in moral and spiritual matters, allied with a rejection of institutional life, both in the Churches and in secular society as well. The shift is most marked in the younger generation, though disillusionment with the major institutions of our society is certainly not confined to the young. For the Churches, one disturbing consequence of this distancing from institutions is that belief tends to become more and more detached from any of the traditional forms, and thus more personal and idiosyncratic. In this sense Clifford Longley is right to say that public faith is much less of a reality to the under-40s than to earlier generations, when the institutional links were stronger and folk religion was closer to something vaguely resembling orthodoxy.

But this is not the whole picture. Older people have always been more religious than the young. It is possible that we are experiencing a marked generational shift with respect to religious understanding and behaviour, but we cannot yet be certain of this. If, as seems to be happening, there is a growing demand for good religious education in schools, and a growing popularity of Church schools, and growing competition from other faiths, it is possible that *more* of the basic elements of religion may be conveyed to the next generation than has been conveyed in the recent past.

On top of this generational problem, we have to recognise the widespread change in consciousness in the direction of post-modernism: the shift from duty to self-fulfilment, from truth to opinion, from community to individual, from the understanding of a comprehensive tradition to transitory insights. These shifts are not just the prerogative of the chattering classes. They have permeated our culture more deeply than that, partly through the political climate of recent years, but also as one of the consequences of the information explosion. There are simply too many things to react to, to assimilate, to challenge our own ideas, and to disorientate us. Saturation by the media encourages a kaleidoscopic kind of consciousness. The idea that there may be public and unassailable truths and values becomes hard to entertain. And with this loss comes not so much a failure of nerve as a loss of a sense of shared landmarks and of direction.

Yet the longing for something more enduring persists. Jonathan Sacks, in his writings about the importance of the moral law as the basis for community and family life, has won plaudits from people (including Clifford Longley) who in varying degrees sense the dangers of becoming locked into the kind of culture I have just been describing. He reinforces the point that, even if the sketch I have given is a fair description of what has been happening to our society, this is not the moment to abandon the attempt to build up a public faith and morality; in fact, it is the moment to try even harder. Grace Davie quotes a moving passage from David Martin describing the role of the Church in such a culture:

> We in England live in the chill religious vapours of northern Europe, where moribund religious establishments loom over populations that mostly do not enter churches for active worship even if they entertain inchoate beliefs. Yet these establishments guard and maintain thousands of houses of God, which are markers of space and time. Not only are they markers and

45

anchors, but also the only repositories of all-embracing meanings pointing beyond the immediate to the ultimate. They are the only institutions that deal in tears and concern themselves with the breaking points of human existence. They provide frames and narratives and signs to live by, and offer persistent points of reference. They are repositories of signs about miraculous birth and redemptive sacrifice, shared tables and gift-giving; and they offer moral codes and exemplars for the creation of communal solidarity and the nourishment of virtue. They are places from which to launch initiatives which help sustain the kind of networks found, for example, in the inner city; they welcome schools and regiments and rotary clubs; they celebrate and commemorate; they are islands of quietness; they are places in which unique gestures occur of blessing, distribution and obeisance; they offer spaces in which solemnly to gather, to sing, to lay flowers, and light candles. They are – in Philip Larkin's phrase – serious places on serious earth.

Theological

That quotation brings me to what I want to say from a theological perspective. I begin with the now familiar description of the Church as sign, instrument and foretaste of the kingdom of God. To think of the Church simply as a kind of social cement, an undergirding for the values on which public life depends, is to miss all the subtlety of that description. It is to lose the sense of fundamental tension between Church and society which is inherent in the message of the cross.

The Church, as a sign of meaning in a bleak and unfriendly world, is all that David Martin says it is. It should affirm an ultimate hope, in the light of the cross and resurrection, and thus provide an environment in which many lesser hopes can flourish and many otherwise struggling human endeavours can be affirmed. A large part of an archbishop's job, for instance, is to go round giving encouragement, not by vacuous back-slapping, but by setting good things in their divine context.

But the Church should also be a sign of contradiction, a critic, an awkward customer, an exposer of evil and injustice, a reminder of judgement. I am conscious that Anglicanism is on the whole better at affirming than at criticising, and this is one reason why I am a passionate ecumaniac. We actually need a variety of witnesses, a variety of experiences, if the diverse forms of Christian social witness, and the tensions within such witness, are to be expressed. It is essential, though, that this variety should exist within a single Christian fellowship, and not simply in the differences between separate Churches. My experience of ecumenical working is that it enables the Church to be a sign of affirmation and a sign of contradiction simultaneously, both pointing to that which lies beyond the Church, the Kingdom of God which is, and is to be.

The Church should also be an instrument of the Kingdom, and that must surely mean involvement in the ambivalences of social and political action. Charles Davis in his book *Religion and the Making of Society* goes so far as to claim that social and political action is now the sole valid means of expressing the Christian Gospel. He distinguishes between what he calls the three worlds of modern culture: the objective world of human knowledge, the social world of practice with its norms, and the subjective world of self-awareness. Our apprehensions of transcendence relate to all three in terms of cosmic religion, political religion and contemplative religion. Nowadays, he says, knowledge is too fragmented to provide any standing-ground for the kind of cosmic synthesis which sustained medieval faith. By the same token, we now have other ways of exploring the depths of human consciousness, and there is not necessarily anything peculiarly religious about inwardness, vital though inwardness can be as a vehicle for religious experience. By contrast, the Christian religion has always been concerned with action, and it is much more characteristic of Christianity to find God in our neighbour than to find him in our inner consciousness, or in the cosmos.

I have compressed what is already a compressed argument, and Davis would be the first to admit that he overstates his case. Actual Christian experience contains all three of the elements I have been describing. But he may well be right in giving a central place to action, not as part of a desperate attempt to be relevant, but in recognition of the truth that Christianity has always been political, just

47

as the acts of God have always been in the broadest sense political. What has so often gone wrong with Christian political action is not that it has been political, but that it has been inept, and has lost touch with the basic Christian imperatives.

Thus far Charles Davis. I have dwelt on him because there is a case here to be answered by critics who would want to take Christianity out of the public sphere, or who despair of trying to articulate a publicly relevant faith. Our culture may be exerting powerful pressures in the direction of privatisation, but I do not see how this could possibly be acquiesced in by those who see the Church as an instrument of the Kingdom, or by any who call themselves Catholic.

On the Church as a foretaste of the Kingdom of God, I will only say that this leads us straight to the much-discussed topic of community. It is fundamental to our understanding of Catholic Christianity that human fulfilment is not found in individualism, but in our relationship with each other and with God. I always recall the story of the somewhat overzealous saint who was greeted at the gates of heaven with the question, 'Where are the others?' To stress community is not in itself an argument for the public dimension of faith. There are communities quite happy to keep themselves to themselves. But the call to community points us in the direction of public faith, if 'the others' whom we must bring with us are those who flounder in our society because it seems to lack sense and purpose.

Let me repeat. I strongly believe that it is an important task of the Church to undergird that search for sense and purpose in a society, unless the society is itself so rotten that it has to be abandoned. And the Church does this through the affirmation of what is good, through the identification of, and opposition to, what is wrong, through social and political action, and through the quality of its own life as a community. All this remains its responsibility, even though the particular culture in which we now live may be unreceptive.

European

I come thirdly to the European context in which our present
English culture needs to be understood. The most obvious
retort to Clifford Longley's identification of a peculiar English malaise is that it is by no means unique. There is
enough evidence in the European Value Systems Study to
show that the social changes which afflict us in Britain are
common to Western Europe as a whole. David Martin,
lecturing earlier this year to the Northern Church Leaders,
spoke about a strongly secular belt running diagonally
across Europe from Berlin to Birmingham, through the
most highly fragmented and individualised regions of European society, and drawing no distinction between Catholic
and Protestant areas.

My own contacts with the European Churches, particularly in relation to the European Union, have revealed a
similar picture. Britain may differ from other European
countries in its political attitudes, but socially and cul-
turally we all face much the same problems.

Last year I lectured to a group of university dons and
politicians in Leuven on the subject of the Anglican Church
and the unification of Europe. I think they were somewhat
bemused by my exploration of different models of unity,
from the Commonwealth and the Anglican Communion to
the Council of Churches for Great Britain and Ireland. They
were in no doubt about their own relatively uncomplicated
approach to European union, and it was not hard to see
why. I had a longish conversation, for instance, with a
German living in Luxembourg who works in Belgium.
Frontiers, languages and currencies meant nothing to him.
Most of the Central European countries have had constant
changes to their borders. Belgium itself is a fairly recent
invention, with such a weak sense of national identity that
the Belgians I have spoken to seem to contemplate with
equanimity its possible division into two separate countries. Many Germans, despite their social and economic
successes, still suffer from huge self-doubt, and see European union as in part a protection against themselves. Geo-
graphically and historically the contrast with Britain could
not be greater, and I find it much more plausible to link

49

differing political perceptions of Europe to these factors rather than to some unique English malaise.

I wonder, for instance, what the recent wrapping up of the Reichstag says about the respect for political institutions in Germany, a country where obedience to authority is much more highly rated than in Britain. Indeed, political life in most Western European countries seems at a lower ebb, and in some of them much more dangerously unstable, than in Britain. The Germans have been far more generous in their treatment of refugees than we have, but much less generous in giving them citizenship. In probing the reason why, it became obvious that at the root of it is a deep problem about German national identity. But that is a long and different story.

My purpose in giving these examples is not to enter into the argument about European union, but simply to make the point that Western European society as a whole is suffering contradictions and uncertainties, though these may take different forms in different countries. And because in many parts Churches have been closely bound up with the societies within which they belong, the Churches have suffered self-questioning and decline along with the other institutions. This may be an argument against getting too close to the sources of power. It also raises questions, though, about how power has traditionally been distributed. The Church of England may have more of the trappings of power than many continental Churches, but we have not for a long time had a total monopoly of the kind which emerged when continental countries defined themselves at the Reformation by their religious allegiance. The tension between establishment and dissent in England has saved us from the worst excesses of intolerance and anti-clericalism, and has ensured that the national Church has always had vigorous critics from without – and also, healthily, from within. This is a further reason why I believe that ecumenism should nowadays be central to our thinking about Church and society.

The question remains, though, why Western Europe has suffered such a catastrophic decline in Church membership and in institutional life in general. The fact that it is common to the whole of Europe should make us look for deeper causes than the failings of a particular Church. Europe as the home of the Enlightenment, and as the generator of the acids of modernity and the even more corrosive acids of post-modernity, is frequently described as having eroded its own philosophical and moral basis. Too much criticism and too little faith has brought us to the brink of nihilism. Authority has been undermined, in principle during the eighteenth century, and in practice in our own century. Increasing ease of access to information in our own day means that nobody is an authority any more, except individuals with their modems and their computers and with the Internet to supply their needs.

Anti-Enlightenment thinking has been much explored by the Gospel and Our Culture Movement. I remain unconvinced, however, that one can or should try to undo the main achievements of the Enlightenment, and I am sufficiently old-fashioned to believe that faith should be reasonable, and that there are still traditional and well-tested authorities worth trusting. Nevertheless, it is true that there have been, and still are, destructively critical forces at work in European society, and that there is real evidence of a *trahison des clercs* among the guardians of tradition. A relentless search for the new, the shocking, the pin which bursts the bubble, and the fashionable radicalism which grabs the headlines, has penetrated beyond the Sunday supplements deep into the intellectual life of Europe, and to some extent into the churches as well.

My hunch is that all this has had more effect on Western culture than on other cultures for two reasons closely bound up with European history. Europe since Christendom has always had a missionary stance. It has been concerned with universal truths and with universal power. Greek philosophy was believed to have laid down principles of reason and logic which were of universal application, and which still remain essential to science in whatever culture it is practised. The Christian influence on Europe reinforced this sense of a universal mission. Christ transcends all cultures and breaks down all barriers. The Gospel is true for everybody. Whether or not this is expressed in actual missionary endeavour, the perception of universality remains the same. Indeed, that is why we ourselves are here. We are Catholics.

But the sense of mission is not confined to philosophy, science and religion. We have been missionaries in the broadest sense. We have exported Western ways of life to almost every part of the world. African natives in the bush, more likely than not, wear trousers. Papuans listen to transistor radios. I shall never forget going into a Palestinian refugee camp in Beirut in 1981, and finding the children reading Shakespeare.

The claim to universal truth has in the past been uncomfortably close to the exercise of universal power, including fire-power. I do not want in any way to denigrate the century of missionary expansion, but one has only to read history, particularly that of a continent like Africa, to confirm that it depended on guns as well as bibles. There was a degree of arrogance in the assumption that Africa was virgin land waiting to be exploited. We think differently now. We have renounced this kind of power, militarily if not economically. There are profound undercurrents of guilt about some of the abuses of power. There is a growing sense that what Europe has exported to the world, though life-giving in many respects, has also been uncomfortably ambivalent.

In other words, two important assumptions at the heart of European self-consciousness, assumptions about truth and about power, have both been at least partially eroded. Add to this the undermining of authority and the growing spirit of destructive criticism, and I think we can see why Western Europe as a whole lacks self-confidence and shares a common sense of disorientation. The malaise has deep roots in the history we share with other European countries, and in the very achievements of our common culture.

Catholicism

So far I have been trying in a roundabout way to pinpoint some of the factors in our present situation, sociological, theological, and broadly cultural, which all Churches must recognise if they are to relate meaningfully to their social environment. Running through what I have been saying is a subtext about the need for public faith, a faith not exclusive to the Churches themselves, but able to inform, and to some extent guide and sustain, public life. I come finally to the question: What has this to do with Affirming Catholicism?

The intention of Catholic Christianity is to be all-embracing. How can we give expression to this in a society which may need us, but by and large does not want us? How can we, with our sense of the universal, communicate effectively in a society which no longer believes in universals? And how can we sustain our own Catholic identity without falling into the trap of rooting it in peculiar practices, in marks of distinction, a self-chosen Catholic style, which in earlier generations indirectly marked out Catholics as being separate and odd – in other words, not Catholics at all.

I am reminded of a cartoon in which a wife is showing a friend her husband's observatory, where he sits with his eye glued to an enormous telescope. The caption reads: 'This is my husband. He lives in a little world of his own.'

It seems to me that our all-embracingness as Catholics depends more on what we are looking at than on precisely where we stand in relation to all the distinctions and controversies which can occupy us so much in our small ecclesiastical world. What we have to offer is a vision, a hope, and a means of expressing these in worship.

The vision is of an ultimate unity which can contain our present fragmentations because it is itself many-sided and dynamic. Let me try to unpack that as part of the significance of the doctrine of the Trinity. For me one of the theological excitements of our age has been the turning of what could often in the past have seemed a dry, static formula designed to make the best of contradictory historical claims about the nature of God, into the rediscovery of the doctrine which holds within it the living heart of Christian faith. It can give us profound insights into the nature of reality, into our own nature as persons, and into our dependence as persons on our relationship with others.

Though we have a long way to go before we can translate these insights into the clues needed to interpret our present culture, I believe the possibility is there. Just to give one example, it seems to me that the doctrine provides the most promising way of tackling issues about the uniqueness of Christianity in relation to other faiths. This is an explosive issue which raises all the hard questions about universal claims made in a pluralist culture. But if we ask what it means that the Spirit proceeds from the Father as well as from the Son, we might be able to identify works of the Spirit which, though ultimately centred on the second person of the Trinity, are not exclusively linked to the incarnation. And this leads on to the further question: Can we recognise the Spirit of God even where Christ is not named? The doctrine of the Trinity opens up a range of subtleties in talking about God which may be hugely valuable in an age when we tend to be overwhelmed by the variety and contradictoriness of human experience.

In pursuing our vision, we need to take more seriously the widespread consciousness of a transcendent dimension to life, the search for some kind of spirituality among people who reject traditional religion. A grasp of the complex dynamism of Trinitarian faith, of the nearness and the mystery of God, of his presence beyond us and within us, can save us from the simplistic images which are instantly and rightly dismissed. Catholicism tells us of a big God who is present in unexpected places.

Hope, perhaps even more than vision, is needed in an age when vision is all too frequently derided, or all too quickly overtaken by the next fashion. I have been slightly put out by numerous recent headlines proclaiming 'Hope for York', as if it was in particularly short supply in this diocese. But I am comforted by the thought that, since Moltmann, hope is now one of our key theological categories. I believe it is also central to the understanding of Catholicism.

I have always seen Catholicity more as a goal for the future than as a gift from the past. I rather doubt whether there ever was a complete Catholic past any more than there was a time when the Church was completely united. Christianity was an explosion of new life and new ideas, flowing out in all directions, gradually creating forms of unity, then losing them and rediscovering them, but always conscious of differences, and finding it hard to let go of traditions once they had become the vehicles of this life. The very fact that the need for unity is so constantly stressed in the New Testament is evidence that from the beginning it was hard to achieve. To my mind it is quite impossible to read the New Testament as if the Gospel were a carefully designed package handed over by Jesus, and simply needed to be passed on. There was variety and dissension from the very first. Though in one sense everything had happened in the cross and the resurrection, they also knew that it was simply a beginning, and that in some sense the Body of Christ still had to be fashioned. So they looked forward in hope.

To see the Church in this way is not to underrate the classic marks of Catholicity. These emerged out of history, and they are not to be ignored. They define the road. They are not some sort of ticket, nor do they define the destination. Difficulties and deviations on the journey need not invalidate the ultimate hope. Every time we read the Psalms we are reminded of how the Jews lived primarily by hope. They experienced the destruction of almost all they valued, yet they went on in hope. Though as Christians we say that their hope was fulfilled in Christ, we recognise that we too have to live in hope until Christ is all in all. In hope we can face the fact that we live in lean times. In hope it is possible to accept and work with the fragmentariness and transitoriness of much of today's social scene, because we have no mandate to claim a unity and a certainty which human beings will not possess this side of the end.

We do, however, possess a means, and this is why I want to end with a brief word about the significance of Catholic sacramentalism in the context I have been attempting to describe. As sacramentalists we have it laid upon us to take the whole created order seriously. It is basic to our faith that creation contains within itself the possibilities of revealing and conveying the divine. But we actually see this happening only on a small scale – in individual lives, in particular acts of worship, in elements set aside for this particular purpose. I have written elsewhere about 'making sense' as at the same time both an act of discovery and an act of creation. When it is hard for us to make our universal

4 What Sort of Unity for What Sort of Mission?*

Mary Tanner

I begin with a very personal story. It is the story of one of those moments of disclosure that stand out in my ecumenical experience. It was a meeting of the Faith and Order Commission of the World Council of Churches in January 1982 in Lima, Peru. About 120 theologians from many different Churches were staying together in a Roman Catholic retreat centre on the outskirts of the town. In that barren country, where it hardly ever rains, we were enclosed in a beautiful oasis. A stream ran through the centre of the campus, trees and plants blossomed around us. For years the Faith and Order Commission had worked to formulate a text setting out all that could be said together on baptism, Eucharist and ministry. The moment came when the text was completed. Nikos Nissiotis, the Greek Orthodox theologian, Moderator of Faith and Order, asked, 'Is this text mature enough to go to the Churches?' The question received unanimous assent. In silence the group stood up to give thanks for what was, on any reckoning, a significant step on the road to Christian unity.[1]

Looking out of the window in that time of silence I saw that we were enclosed in our comfortable, Eden-like oasis by a high, barbed-wire-covered wall. Outside, the barren hills rose on every side. Where the scrubby plants gave way to desert were a few small shacks, mostly half-built, where the poor, unimaginably poor, eke out some sort of living. The Church was there in its comfortable, secure oasis, safeguarding its life-giving gifts of baptism, Eucharist and ministry, while outside was a world of poverty, star-

*© Mary Tanner 1996

vation and death. Unless what we were doing in searching for Christian unity had something, no, everything to do with that world – God's world – theological table-talk was indulgent and irrelevant. The unity of the Church is not an end in itself. We are not called to be a holy huddle, immune from the pain and anguish of the world, but out there in the midst of it all, strengthened together by the gifts of grace we were struggling to apprehend and holding out those gracious gifts to all. The unity of the Church is to witness to the possibility of healing and unity for all people. The Church is to be the world ahead of itself pointing in its own life to the Kingdom. Unity and evangelism belong together.

It therefore makes little sense to me to explore the Church's task of evangelism without somewhere in the mix of these days holding evangelism together with the search for Christian unity. This linking of mission and evangelism with the search for unity is surely hospitable to those who identify themselves as Catholics and who want to affirm Catholicism. I have recently re-read George Tavard's book *The Quest for Catholicity* in which Tavard traces the passion for Catholicity in the Anglican tradition, through Gardiner, the Catholic Divines, to the Oxford Movement and on into the twentieth century.[2] His survey demonstrates how a concern for unity – a unity with the Church of old, a blessed unity of heart and mind with existing communities and a prospective unity with a progression on earth – belong together in the Anglican-Catholic tradition with a concern for Catholicity. The concern for Catholicity includes the capacity of the one Church to encompass all humanity, not just one or another nation but all humanity in every place and every time. Unity and evangelism or mission belong inextricably together in this Catholic view of things.

A second conviction underlies what I have to say. While it is fashionable to talk of ecumenical winter, of an ecumenical movement which has stopped moving, and to emphasise despondency and frustration, I discern in the last months quite the reverse. There is an 'ecumenical moment' dawning, and this ecumenical moment ought to be nurtured by those who are concerned to affirm Catholicism, for what is emerging in this ecumenical moment is hospitable to Catholicism and holds out a possibility for strengthening the mission and evangelism of the Church.

A third conviction is that there are areas in the understanding of what sort of unity evangelism requires that need creative thought and clarification. Those who are committed to affirming the Catholicity of the Church have something very particular to contribute to the emerging portrait of the unity we seek to live with all Christians.

Let us now look in detail at these three convictions: that unity and evangelism are inextricably bound together; that there is a special ecumenical moment as we approach the end of the ecumenical century; and that there is need for creative imagination to develop an understanding of what sort of unity evangelism requires.

Unity and Evangelism Belong Together

'Evangelism is the communication of the good news of Christ's Kingdom and his accompanying command to people to repent, believe and be baptised into his body of the Church.'[3] This is the succinct definition of evangelism given by the bishops at the 1988 Lambeth Conference when the bishops called for a Decade of Evangelism. It is a useful, short definition as far as it goes. It emphasises the content of the message of evangelism – the proclamation of Christ's Kingdom. It makes clear that evangelism is not just an individual matter but to do with the community of the Church, about a call to baptism into the body of Christ, the Church. In this definition, believing and belonging are held together. The Church is the company of the evangelised and is entrusted with the task of evangelism. The evangelised are to be the evangelisers.

What this definition does not draw out, however, is that the good news of Christ's Kingdom is proclaimed in our words, in our deeds and in our very being. Evangelism is about helping people to hear the Gospel, not just by hearing the words of good news, but through seeing the good news of the Kingdom incarnated, embodied in us. Evangelism is not only, not even primarily, about preaching. It is about ordering our lives in such a way that there is some chance

59

that those whose lives touch ours will glimpse in us the Kingdom of God: that they will see in us the signs of the Kingdom and recognise a possibility for their own lives. A recent survey on 'finding faith' shows that people become Christians in the main through being attracted to something they see in others, not by words spoken to or at them.

The sad fact is that the credibility of our message of the unity of God's Kingdom, a gift for all, goes on being obscured by the division of the Churches. As long as we are happy to coexist in divisions, even if we are prepared for co-operation and commitment, then we are a counter-sign to the unity and peace of God's Kingdom. As long as Christians are divided we neither experience ourselves the gift of Catholicity, nor can we offer an experience of God's promise to others. As long as we are divided around the eucharistic table we fail to offer credibly Christ's invitation to the one banquet in the Kingdom of Heaven at which all are invited to eat and drink. As long as we are divided our resources for service, for binding up the world's wounds, are competitive and less effective. As long as we are divided, far from bringing in the unity of God's Kingdom, we actually contribute to the divisions and disunity of the world. The divisions between the Churches have been responsible for some of the darkest moments in the world's history. We see it close to home in Ireland and we see it in the anguish of the present situation in Bosnia. If the barriers between Churches of East and West, Orthodox and Roman Catholic, had been broken down and if unity of faith and life had been restored then the Church might have played its part in stabilising the situation, pointing through its own life to a Kingdom of justice, peace and unity. Christian disunity is a stumbling block to the task of evangelism to which we are called.

An Ecumenical Moment of Possibility

The Church's task of evangelism, its proclamation of the good news of the Kingdom, is weakened by the failure of those who have been entrusted with the Gospel message to be united amongst themselves. It is for this reason that we ought to be alert and responsive to any reawakening of a desire for Christian unity, any movement to make more visible the unity of the Church. I hope I am not mistaken, but it does seem to me remarkable that, after the despondency and frustration of past failures, there are signs now of a new desire for unity being expressed in many places.

I see it in the growth of local ecumenical partnerships in Britain where, at best, Christians discover it is better together and where the motivation to face and overcome the burden of structural difficulties of coming together is the commitment to united witness and service to the local community. There is no more powerful testimony to this than in the books by David Shepherd and Derek Worlock, *Better Together* and *With Hope in Our Hearts*.[4] The call to unity can be detected in the rush of invitations to the Church of England to enter new unity conversations. How else can be explained the fact that, in spite of our track record and rebuttals, the Moravians, the Free Church of England, the Baptists, the URC and the Methodists have each invited us to talks to consider moving into closer communion? How else can such moves towards the Church of England by those who have been bruised by us be accounted for than from a reawakening of a desire for unity? Dr Lesley Griffiths, a past president of the Methodist Conference, forcefully and honestly (too bluntly for some) wrote to the press recently about the need for a united witness because our divisions continue as a stumbling block for the work God calls us to do. However, he left us in no doubt that he feared the will or the ability of the Church of England to respond. It is salutary to listen to how he sees us:

> I have come to despair of the apathy, hostility, legalism, aloofness and caution which strew the way towards the realisation of what is, after all, the command of Jesus *ut unum sint*. Indeed, I now feel that there will be no significant progress in my lifetime, if at all. If that turns out to be the case, I can only conclude that the Church of Jesus Christ will have succeeded once again in belittling God with its own littleness.[5]

The Church of England must listen to this criticism and own up to its failures to co-operate – the closing of theological colleges without consultation, the going it alone in producing reports that could better be produced together.

The desire for Christian unity can be seen in the approaches to the Church of England of Churches in Continental Europe. The motivation is the conviction that Christian unity in Europe would contribute to a Europe seeking for its own coherence and stability. Since the 1930s the Church of England has had a close relationship with the Old Catholic Church, through the Bonn Agreement. It is time to make that relationship more effective. Since 1991 it has been in an agreement, the Meissen Agreement, with the German Churches. That agreement is having practical consequences in many ways. Currently, Anglicans in Britain and Ireland are engaged in talks with the French Lutheran and the Reformed Churches. Since the vote of the General Synod in July 1995, the Porvoo Agreement has brought Anglicans in Scotland, England and Ireland (Wales has yet to vote) into full visible unity with some of the Nordic and Baltic Lutheran Churches. The title of the Porvoo Report, *Together in Mission and Ministry*, shows that the impetus for this development comes from a perceived need for a common mission and evangelism in northern Europe.

> Our Churches are called together to proclaim the Christian hope arising from faith, which gives meaning in societies characterised by ambiguity. They are called together to proclaim the healing love of God and reconciliation in communities wounded by persecution, oppression and injustice. This common proclamation in word and sacrament manifests the mystery of God's love, God's presence and God's Kingdom.[6]

The desire for unity can also be seen in the recent encyclical of the pope, *Ut unum sint*, with its call to the Churches of the East and the Churches of the West.[7] 'Full unity', the pope says, 'is part of evangelisation, and lack of it has damaged Christian Churches.' The text is remarkable for its open recognition of the part the Roman Catholic Church has played in contributing to Christian divisions, and in its begging for forgiveness. In a quite unprecedented way the pope asks for the help of other Churches in understanding the vocation of the Petrine ministry in the service of the unity of the whole Church. It is a task he freely admits he cannot undertake alone. The pope invites a dialogue in which, leaving past controversies behind, we could listen to one another, keeping before us only the will of Christ for his Church and allowing ourselves to be deeply moved by Christ's plea 'that they may be one ... so the world may believe'.

So at the local level, at the national level, at the European level and at the world level there can be detected quite remarkably an ecumenical moment, a possibility for greater wholeness. The cynics will say that in England this is a response to declining numbers and diminishing financial resources; that in Europe it is no more than a pan-Protestant alliance to hold at bay a re-evangelising of Europe by a Catholic pope and that the seeming generosity of *Ut unum sint* is only a weapon to get us all to capitulate to an unreformed papacy. But there is a more optimistic reading of the signs of the times. The drives for unity come from a genuine desire for *metanoia* – a turning to Christ and a turning to one another in Christ. They come from a genuine desire to be more faithful witnesses to the reconciliation and unity of the Kingdom for the sake of the Church's credibility in its evangelistic task.

If there is a moment of ecumenical promise then Christians are challenged to affirm it with all the charity, humility and determination that can be mustered. For to make more visible the unity of the Church would be to be more credible and effective in our evangelistic task. Here is a particular challenge for the Church of England, and here is a particular challenge for those in the Catholic tradition, for the sort of unity that is being affirmed by the Church of England in an agreement like the Porvoo Agreement is a unity which is totally consistent with those things that Catholic Anglican tradition has sought to safeguard since the Reformation. The Porvoo portrait of unity is that 'the unity of the Church is given in Christ and rooted in the Triune God'. The ecclesiology of Porvoo is grounded in the understanding of the *koinonia*, communion of God's own trinitarian life, with its christological centre and Spirit dynamic. This is the mystery of the Church.

The Archbishop of York ended his discussion of the

Church in society in the previous chapter by saying that
he believed that the movement to take the doctrine of
the Trinity into our understanding of living the heart of the
Christian faith is the single most important thing happening in our understanding of things today. The archbishop
began to throw out some clues of what this might mean
for understanding the relation of Christianity to other faiths
and for our life together in the community of the Church.
It is similarly a concentration on the doctrine of the Trinity
which is having the profoundest effect on ecumenical
ecclesiology and on the understanding of the unity we seek
to live with all Christian men and women. The goal of
unity is being reinterpreted and re-visioned by an understanding of *koinonia*.[8] The Porvoo portrait of unity is
described thus:

> The unity of the Church given in Christ and rooted in the Triune
> God is realised in our unity in the proclaimed word, the sacra-
> ments and the ministry instituted by God and conferred through
> ordination. It is lived both in the unity of faith to which we
> jointly witness, and which together we confess and teach, and
> in the unity of hope and love which leads us to unite in fully
> committed fellowship. Unity needs a visible outward form
> which is able to encompass the element of inner differentiation
> and spiritual diversity as well as the element of historical
> change and development. This is the unity of a fellowship which
> covers all times and places and is summoned to witness and
> serve the world.[9]

Anglicans are committed to living with Lutheran partners in northern Europe a unity in faith, a common faith
grounded in Holy Scriptures, set forth in the Catholic
creeds; a unity in worship and sacramental life; a unity in
the ministry of the whole people of God served by a single
ordered ministry in threefold form, and a unity held
together and served by collegial and communal structures.
Historic episcopal succession is part of this shared life and
an inescapable feature of visible unity. Historic episcopal
succession is not an optional extra, but neither is it a
guarantee of any Church's fidelity. It is a sign of God's
promise to be with his Church and a sign of the Church's
intention to remain faithful to its apostolic calling. The

agreement has succeeded in finding a generous way of affirming historic episcopal succession without denying the apostolicity of another episcopal Church which has not understood historic episcopal succession in quite the way we have.

How very close all of this is to what has been handed on in the Anglican Catholic tradition, with its insistence that the visible Church is the embodiment of Christ – the extension of the incarnation; that the visible institution of the Church coheres with the incarnation; and that the institutions of Scripture, creeds, the sacraments and a ministry of apostolic authority in apostolic continuity are its 'covenanted channels and instruments of grace', to quote Bishop Gore.

Here is an ecumenical moment and an ecumenical possibility hospitable to the Catholic Anglican tradition. It deserves to be nurtured and offered to others, for by making more visible the unity of the Church we shall be more faithful to our call to evangelism.

Deepening the Portrait of Unity

There remain huge areas to be explored if we are to get hold at a deeper level of the sort of unity evangelism requires if the Church is to become more faithfully the sign of the Kingdom. One of the things we need to work for is to deepen the understanding of what it means for the Church to be *sign*. The Archbishop of York has written of the Church as sign, instrument and foretaste of the Kingdom, a familiar theme in ecumenical discussion. The Bishop of Salisbury has developed the same theme in his chapter in this book, 'Evangelism and Worship'. In his Introduction the Bishop of Edinburgh has written of the Old Testament missionary model as a model of magnetism, which is also paradigmatic for the Church.

If our unity is to point others to the Kingdom of God then our life as Christians together must show that, however much we value the structural and ordered life of the Church, the personal and relational are always prior to the institutional and structural. We shall not be a sign of the Kingdom of God unless we reveal those qualities in the community of the Church of which the New Testament speaks: patience, forbearance, trust, above all love. St Paul emphasises in his Letters the qualities of the life in unity. In Ephesians 4, when he speaks of one body, one Lord, one faith, one baptism, Paul begins his reflection on unity by calling Christians to be humble, gentle, patient, putting up with one another's failings in the spirit of love. Personal and relational attitudes are the living tissue of our unity and a sign to the world of the peace and unity of God's Kingdom.

If unity is to point others to the Kingdom of God then it must be a unity that astonishes with its diversity. Diversity is not a concession to the life of the Church but the out-working of a life grounded in the life of the Holy Trinity. But this is not the diversity of denominations brought together in some loose federation. The unity we offer to the world is not some reconciled diversity where denominations live side by side, holding hands over the barriers of separation, but a diversity which exists in a single fellow-ship, within an organic unity. This unity does not call for the sacrifice of diversity of expressions of revealed truth, nor spiritualities, disciplines, expressions of ministry or liturgical rites. Confidence in the covenanted means of grace makes for confidence in the blossoming of diverse expressions of faith, life and witness. Of course there are limits to diversity, and a part of living together in unity requires being prepared to explore continuously what those limits might be.

If unity is to point others to that Kingdom of God then it will always be a community holding together in dialogue and exploration. The faith of the Church grounded in Holy Scripture, confessed in the symbols of the Catholic creeds, borne witness to in the traditions of all the Churches, has to be expressed afresh in and for each generation. Contem-porary experience helps us to discover new things in the tradition: the tradition sometimes helps to confirm our con-temporary experience, sometimes to judge it. One of the most important ecumenical (and not only ecumenical) debates is on trying to find a common understanding of hermeneutics – not only about the Bible but how to inter-pret Christian inheritance as guidance for contemporary

Christian living. If we could make progress here we should understand much more of what it means to be together in unity – a community of dialogue and exploration. We must be prepared to risk living together with the provisional, for the truth of God and God's Kingdom is so intimately complex, delicately balanced and wonderfully subtle. Truth, the truth of the Kingdom, can never be trapped in hard-edged, inflexible moulds. We dare not offer funda-mentalist certainties. The same Gospel story has to be told, the same credal symbols recited, the same sacramental grace received, but these must be constantly reinterpreted, linguistically and conceptually. The reinterpretation is itself proof that the one apostolic tradition is alive and relevant in the world today.

If unity is to point to the Kingdom of God then it must allow that this side of that Kingdom disagreements, tension, even conflict will be a part of our Christian life together. It was Elizabeth Templeton who helped the bishops at the 1988 Lambeth Conference to see this, as they struggled with the issue of the ordination of women to the episcopate.

> Sharp things that divide us can paradoxically turn out to be gift. The world with all its divisions is not used to such a possibility as this: that those on opposing sides should stay together, should remain in dialogue, bearing each other's burden, even entering one another's pain.

Perhaps we are learning something of this in the Church of England in the painful struggle to uphold the integrity of those on both sides of the debate on women's ordination, as we hold together in the crucible of change and develop-ment, acknowledging a degree of incompleteness and pro-visionality. In a strange way this may be a powerful contribution to contemporary evangelism.

If unity is to point to the Kingdom of God then our life of unity must never be turned in on itself, obsessively concerned to preserve its own life apart from the messiness of the world. The Church is to live turned outwards, always ready to risk moving out expecting to find God in the world ahead of us. The Church is bearer of the Gospel –

but the Gospel is also brought to us by and through the world.

If unity is to point to the Kingdom of God then we shall always be seeking to renew our life together. We are swift to recognise and condemn the brokenness of human community in the world; we are so slow to acknowledge human divisions penetrating and distorting the internal life of the Church. The story of women's traditional role in the Church illustrates this only too well. Human divisions of women and men, black and white, rich and poor, employed and unemployed, old and young, do physically affect our lives together, they colour the words we use to celebrate our faith, the way we carry out our ministry, the way we exercise authority. Only a Church which is prepared to devote the time and imagination that Paul devoted to the division of Jew and Gentile to the new divisions of its own day is likely to be an authentic witness to the Kingdom of God. For that effective witness to the Kingdom means that we have constantly to be renewed into unity.

I end where I began. A passion for evangelism and a passion for unity belong together. We proclaim the Good News and attract others to the Kingdom not only by the words we speak but by what we are. A life of unity is a part of the Church's way of being a sign, a prophetic sign of the unity of the Kingdom that God wills to offer through us to all. There is a special ecumenical moment opening up hospitable to Catholic Anglicans, to which those who affirm Catholicism should respond and in which they can take a lead. Further, Catholic Anglicans have a very special contribution to make to envisioning the sort of unity that we seek, and to developing an understanding of what sort of unity is required, and for what sort of mission.

Notes

1 *Baptism, Eucharist and Ministry*, The Lima Text, Faith and Order Paper No. 111, WCC, 1982.

2 G. Tavard, *The Quest for Catholicity*, Herder & Herder, 1964.

3 *The Truth Shall Make You Free*, The Lambeth Conference, ACC, 1988, p. 43.

4 D. Sheppard and D. Worlock, *Better Together*, Hodder & Stoughton, 1988, and *With Hope in Our Hearts*, Hodder & Stoughton, 1994.
5 *Church Times*, June 1995.
6 *The Porvoo Common Statement*, Conversations between the British and Irish Anglican Churches and the Nordic and Baltic Lutheran Churches, CCU Occasional Paper No. 3, 1994.
7 *Ut unum sint*, Encyclical Letter of Pope John Paul II on Commitment to Ecumenism.
8 *On the Way to Fuller Koinonia*, Report of the Fifth World Conference on Faith and Order, Faith and Order Paper No. 166, WCC, 1994.
9 *The Porvoo Common Statement*, para. 26.

5 The Flickering Image: Evangelism in an Age of Mass Media*

Angela Tilby

Down in the Duplex: an everyday story of BBC religious media folk.

Episode 1

At the southern end of the lower half of the steel, glass and plasterboard Portakabin, the *Lives of Jesus* team are working. Their space is a little haven of theological calm in the midst of the ferment generated by the production teams of *Heart of the Matter* and *Everyman*. The *Lives of Jesus* is the most ambitious series of programmes about the historical Jesus attempted on British television.

Duplex 2 is a shared home. Our aetiological myth suggests that the Portakabin was brought in its two layers by a very large lorry and erected (no one can remember quite when) in the car park of New Broadcasting House, Manchester.

Sometimes the series producer of the *Lives of Jesus* wonders whether the duplex will be removed by a mysterious visitation, like a thief in the night, and all the VDUs, tape machines, budgets, green plants and telephones with voice mail that she has never mastered the use of – which is why even if I ever give you my telephone number don't expect to be able to communicate with me – will have gone for ever into the dark. She begins for the first time to understand eschatology.

*© Angela Tilby 1996

Given that it rains a lot in Manchester the more likely scenario is that the duplex will simply float away down the Oxford Road, past the university, where there are scholars who believe in Q (remember Q? It's back). Then on to Rusholme, Fallowfield, past Holy Trinity, Platt, with its Evangelical pulpit, past Holy Innocents, the Affirming Catholicism Church, and out past Emmanuel, Didsbury, home of the Radio 4 Long Wave Daily Service, on to Tesco's and the great motorways beyond.

All of which is to say that like many, perhaps most, of those who belong to the middle classes in this country, those of us who work in the media live with a new atmosphere of dislocation, impermanence and fragmentation. I believe that this atmosphere actually permeates the whole of our common life. The non-middle classes have known it for much longer. It produces in all of us a background hum of anxiety, as we are tempted to stabs of ruthlessness or despair in our attempts to survive.

Where, in all this, is the story of Jesus, the old, old story? What cultural space does it occupy? What is the Gospel for this age? And how is the Gospel message heard?

From the perspective of mass journalism the cultural marginalisation of the Church is all too obvious. Though we have friends and well-wishers, sometimes in high places, we are not doing all that well. Our scandals and divisions are embarrassing, even when they are highly entertaining. The perception of decline is backed by facts. Since the early 1960s half the adult members of the Church of England have walked away and not been replaced.

Church and culture seem to have fallen apart. Let me be anecdotal for a moment. When I read theology at Cambridge I was taught exclusively by male clergy, the vast majority of whom were priests of the Church of England. When I joined the Religious Broadcasting Department of the BBC the two most senior management positions were held by Church of England priests, though the ecumenical range was much wider. Most of my Cambridge teachers and BBC bosses were *passing through* academic life or radio and television. Four became bishops, two became deans, one became a provost. One Roman Catholic colleague also became a bishop after his sojourn in the BBC.

71

Now the situation is very different. The Divinity Faculty of Cambridge has been laicised. There are no more chairs tied to canonries at Ely. It is poised to expand as a centre for the advanced study of world religions. The people who work there are not passing through. They want to make their careers there. If they *do* move on it is to Harvard or Oxford or to a redbrick chair. Much less often do they go to a diocese or a deanery. To be successful as academics they have to generate articles, reviews and, above all, big, thick, meaty books. The appointments system in our universities passes over the original but contemplative scholar and the scholar who is moving on and out, in favour of the highly industrious, visible ones.

This shift has a parallel in the media. We no longer recruit the promising young curate who did so well in the Footlights. We look now to journalists, to those who work in local radio, in other words to media professionals, to make our programmes.

I was unusual in 1973 because I was a lay woman in religious broadcasting. Now I am unusual because I am one of the few religious broadcasters who still regularly goes to church.

Episode 2

The series producer of the *Lives of Jesus* lived for a year upstairs in the upper duplex. She tried to introduce a note of levity by christening this top half of the Portakabin Ascension House, and for a time internal memoranda were addressed to Ascension House without irony or question, since the reference was not entirely understood.

The *Lives of Jesus* team are, in fact, unusually religious and heavyweight theologically. They comprise: one series producer, C of E, Affirming Catholicism. Of the other five, three have had some theological training and three (not the same three) go to church quite often. We are drawn together not because of what we represent religiously, but because we have particular skills in making television programmes. I have a fridge in my office which contains a bottle of gin and, sometimes, a lemon. The *Lives of Jesus* which will emerge from our labours will be a Jesus who is somehow mysteriously negotiated between us, and not only between us: the programme will be presented by Mark Tully, who has his own story to tell and exploration to make. The series is also of interest to those who are paying for it. Ultimately, that means the licence fee payer. In practical terms, it means the commissioning controller, through an executive producer, to whom I am responsible. It also means any other television station or organisation which decides to invest in the series.

The requirement is laid upon me that the *Lives of Jesus* be fresh, radical, innovative. In the lower duplex lie the remains of other fresh, radical and innovative attempts to tell the old, old story. Don Cupitt's *Who was Jesus?*, 1977 (the year Lord Grade fulfilled a promise to the pope and presented Robert Powell as Jesus of Nazareth directed by Zeffirelli). In *Who was Jesus?* the cool, academic Don went to Israel and discovered a Jesus who was a remarkable, but very dead, Jewish Rabbi. Then there was *Jesus: The Evidence*, from London Weekend Television. Its overriding message was that the Christian faith was invented by the Emperor Constantine to boost his imperial authority. Then there was A.N. Wilson's *Jesus before Christ*, 1992. It began with A. N. Wilson before the altar of Rugby School chapel. Dressed as an undertaker, his face twitching with emotion, the former Roman Catholic and Anglo-Catholic believer confessed that he had for ever lost his faith because of recent research into the Jesus of history. However, he still has tremendous admiration for the very human historical Jesus.

These retellings are, I think, of comfort to many of the over-45s. They tap into a widespread loss of commitment, universal claims, overarching stories and the institutions which support them. They present a Jesus who is one of us, in a world where the divinity of Jesus and his humanity seem simply to cancel each other out.

This is a confused generation, vaguely respectful of Christian ethics, scornful of theology. Among it are those who would fight to the last for choral evensong, but would prefer it without what they describe as the religious element. But by 1996 the wheel of time has turned again. In the world of media are the 21-year-olds who, while not attending public school, may well have done a module on world religions in their media studies course at university. Their world view is rather different, not least because they have no idea of what the old, old story is. They sometimes wonder about converting to Roman Catholicism because it is so fashionable. Fresh, radical, surprising. No wonder I feel so tired all the time.

But here is something to note about television. There is an unquenchable thirst for novelty. The eye seems to be the organ of the body which tires most quickly. Television craves the new, the unusual, the quirky, the fresh, the unseen, the shocking, the different. The restlessness with which people flip through the listings, saying, 'It's all so boring' or 'It's all repeats', are expressions of that expectation. If television is not new and immediate, it's useless. Television sometimes seems to be run by individuals who are themselves quirky and unusual. They are experts at anticipating and manipulating public taste and interest. This is something that serious scholars and people of faith find very difficult to understand. We are in a fashion industry. How do we tell the foundational story of our civilisation in an environment like this?

Of course, two groups of people have the answer. They are the academics and the true believers. The true believers are writing me letters, accusing the series before it has been made of reductionism and scepticism. The more sophisticated ones simply disapprove of any kind of historical quest, because they *know* from experience that it will come up with the wrong answers.

The academics have the *right* answers, of course, and, in spite of the fact that television trivialises everything and cannot be trusted, they consider it part of their responsibility to a wider public to put us right. I have had painful sessions with serious theologians on both sides of the Atlantic about who should be in and who should be out. There is a curious venom reserved by Jesus scholars for those with whom they disagree. One realises that the toxic St Jerome has left us with a legacy even in these agnostic days.

But academics and true believers, even though they think they are detached, are also part of a media world. The true believers are known to the media. They insist that their faith runs against the tide of culture, are not too dissatisfied with being a despised minority. Academics, on the other hand, would rather like to be loved. To be a success you have to write and write. More than anyone else. Dominic Crossan's book *The Historical Jesus* has sold tens of thousands of copies in its paperback edition. It's subtitle, *The Life of a Mediterranean Jewish Peasant*, catches the attention with its irreverence and subversiveness. The publisher's note states that this is 'The first comprehensive determination of who Jesus was, what he said and what he did', a staggering claim to authority and finality. Is this what it means to be fresh, radical and innovative? It seems a long way from the days when Dennis Nineham could at the same time write his devastatingly sceptical commentary on St Mark and quietly say evensong in Keble College chapel.

The world of media is universal and all-embracing. Whether we love it or hate it, it surrounds and envelops us like air. It is an invisible communion of conflicting stories, diverse narratives, silent or noisy struggles for space and ownership, sudden and surprising revelations of common ground. The claims of Catholicism are also worldwide and all-embracing. And the claim for Christ is that he is of universal meaning.

Episode 3

Our Israeli fixer is on the line from Tel Aviv saying that the Armenian patriarch is worried about the title *The 'Lives' of Jesus*, and if we want to film in this particular location we must explain what exactly the title means.

'There *are* four gospels,' murmurs the series producer enigmatically.

I have been trying to understand who owns Jesus, who owns the cultural space in which the Gospel story is told. Within this I have to recognise that what the unbeliever – the Israeli fixer whose country is destined to become a religious theme park, the unsaved and the sinner, the filthy rich, the gifted artist of loathsome personal habits, the undeserving poor – what all these people have to say about Jesus is now part of the story with which we have to do. Martin Scorsese understands this in *The Last Temptation of*

Christ. How can a twentieth-century person *not* speculate about Jesus and sexual experience, marriage and human intimacy? These are questions of crucial importance to us, and the film-maker does what the Church – as Church – cannot do in exposing the issues that belong to us and our salvation. One wonders what would have happened if the 'ownership' of Jesus had stayed in the hands of the Church. I recently saw an extract from a silent movie of the 1920s in which Jesus was depicted walking on the water. He was propelled upwards like a torpedo from the depth of the lake in a gross mixture of piety and sensationalism.

The lorry may come one day and take away the duplex, layer by layer, first the top and then the bottom. We do not own Jesus, or his story – but who does?

It would be very easy to respond to the fragmentation of our culture with bitterness. The history and doctrine of Jesus and the Church are studied by those whose first interest is not a career as a preacher or pastor but research, teaching and writing. The public face of the life of the Churches is presented by those whose first interest is not to serve religious institutions, but to report on an aspect of British life which large numbers of people find entertaining.

At the same time, the secularisation of religion in academic life and the media has not led to the exclusion of the sacred. The longing for the sacred continues to manifest itself in ordinary human language and speech and yearning, not only in the margins of life but in its very centre. There are still many believers, still many who pray, who look for God. It is just that, on Sunday, they have better things to do.

If we are to understand where the sacred is active we must deal first with the fact that there is a bitterness that hovers around us. This bitterness is a part of the same dislocation from which we ourselves may suffer. We are living both *as* and *among* people who feel they have been badly betrayed. Their security is in tatters. Home-owners, parents, the poor who hoped to be looked after from the cradle to the grave, the jobless and those who wake and sleep in fear that their jobs will be the next to go, all feel betrayed, diminished by political and social changes which seem outside our grasp as the economic strength of Europe is overtaken by the new Pacific economies.

It is easy enough to pitch in with our ounce of bitterness on someone else's behalf, if not our own. After all, we are not the rich and privileged or even very well educated any more. How do we develop a theology of culture when we are part of what is wounded?

The great temptation is to work with a model of the Church as a *pure* community: to set the faithful over against the unfaithful, to assume a dynamic of insiders and out-siders, the clean-living against the loose-living. In such a model Jesus Christ becomes a kind of mascot, what David Jenkins used to call 'a cultic idol'. The Church here operates *contra mundum*: gathering the little flock out of this naughty world.

In such a model, what is it that makes the Church different? According to the Scottish theologian Elizabeth Templeton it could be any one of a number of markers.[1] She suggests consciousness of God, moral achievement, social concern, allegiance to particular doctrines. Once you have one or more of these markers you know you are different, you are one of the few. Not only that, you are also charged with a mission to demonstrate your difference, so 'they'll know we are Christians by our love', perhaps by displaying concern for others, or by the social and political witness to one or other particular causes, or by more direct attempts to persuade others to believe or behave differently. In the rhetoric of over-againstness, this is called extending the Kingdom, or preaching the Gospel, or being prophetic.

This is what people expect of the Church, this is the model journalists and politicians have in mind. Of course, the fundamental charge one would make against such a Church is that of hypocrisy. The messenger is never going to be as good as the message. It is an invitation to the media to prise open the gaps between messenger and message.

We make the charge of hypocrisy *now* against our poli-ticians and journalists. We rightly smell the nasty smell of sulphur when members of the cabinet smugly call for a return to family values while other members are walking out on their wives. The gathered model suggests Christian life as a strenuous moral struggle. But 'to those outside' the result of the struggle is not righteousness, but a deeply unattractive self-righteousness. We forget how people, only a generation or so back, are still punished by such models. I remember hearing about the granddaughter of a divorced woman who remembers that her grandmother was told that if she went to church she must sit with her back to the altar. It is not very long in terms of family memories since the Church routinely inflicted humiliations on people who could not keep up to its standards. Those memories are still alive and they circulate and recirculate.

Elizabeth Templeton goes on to suggest that the 'gathered' model is paralysed by the fact of the numbers of people just being human without reference to religion. The Church cannot work out what to do with them, assuming that its role must be to do something. To convince, persuade, or embrace them. Always there is the assumption that truth travels one way: the 'gathered' Church has something to give, to sell, and the role of the 'outsiders' simply to receive gratefully. It is a model which colonises human experience in order to convince others of their need and convert them to itself.

It works. Of course it works. Many of us are products of this restless intrusiveness which belongs to our Western Christian tradition. I am myself. My interest in Christianity as a teenager was because of its promise to boost a wounded ego. As a sixteen-year-old I was as restless and intrusive as they come, blissfully special in my consciousness of being among the saved. I do not despise such needs, or such solutions, it is just that I think they can be like putting plaster over an unwashed wound.

Elizabeth Templeton contrasts the intrusiveness of the model of the Church as a gathered community with the tradition of Eastern Orthodoxy. In many ways Orthodoxy is more worldly and less idealistic than Western Christianity. It is more at ease with the established order and its flaws and distortions.

> The Church *is* the world. It is the world represented in the fullness of its future, which is as a sharer of God's life. It is a

cosmological fact because of Christ's relationship to humanity and cosmos, not an option for people to be persuaded into.[2]

It is a cosmological fact, not an option for people to be persuaded into. Those are the words that stay with me.

The theological grounding of this view of the Church is the incarnation. Elizabeth Templeton suggests that it is our essential humanness which has been penetrated by the incarnate Christ. If we understand this properly, *any of us* represent the human condition, and all are represented by Christ, the new Adam. She goes on to say that this means the boundaries are already broken down between holy and unholy, saints and sinners, religious and unreligious. The Church does not depend for its existence on a club achieving any kind of growth, or keeping up any particular set of standards. The Church matters simply because it addresses the world with questions about life and death, freedom and hope.

She suggests that this model is well expressed in the solidarities of a Greek village which accepts the local prostitute as a member, not an alien, or in the liturgical act of sharing the Eucharist bread outside the Church. I am also aware that there are still some English and perhaps Church of Scotland parishes in which the church and the community are more or less the same thing. Of course, this makes for difficulties in establishing critical distance and dissent. It faces the Churches with a great deal more ambiguity than they would like to have; are they simply baptising culture without the prophetic note?

Yet I am struck by the fact that the Russian Orthodox Church managed to survive 70 years of communism. Of course, it was all a mess. There were strange and shabby deals with the KGB and with state atheism. Yet somehow it kept alive a luminous vision of the transcendent in our midst, the glory of God in a living human being. I find myself wondering whether we disown the glory of Christ as God's face because our own self-esteem is so damaged, or whether it is the vulnerability of Christ that offends our unconfessed desire for omnipotence. Certainly we live in an atmosphere in which the divine Christ is experienced as an assault on our humanity. I think this is why historians

79

and theologians and media people like to tell the story of Jesus in such ways as to ensure that he remains within the scope of our understanding. Jesus for our time is human, not divine. The humanity and divinity are in conflict, and only one side can win. The 'gathered' Christians huddle beneath his divinity, the rest of us are grateful for his humanity. The divinity and the humanity are at war.

Yet here is the total contradiction of that statement. Sitting in Sainsbury's are rows and rows of the sixth and last volume of Susan Howatch's epic series about the Church of England, *Absolute Truths*. Towards the end, as the rich mix of scandal and spirituality winds towards its conclusion, the narrator of this volume, Charles Ashworth, speaks.

> The moonlight intermingled with the darkness of the woods, just as the candles in the cathedral had intermingled with the darkness of the choir, and as I saw the extravagantly beautiful pattern that was formed I remembered the opening verses of St John's Gospel which described the light sent from God to shine in the darkness and guide flawed humanity along the path to eternal life, that mysterious temporal metaphor which embraced redemption and salvation – and a mode of being which triumphed over time. I thought too, as I reached the brink of the dell and saw the chapel shimmering below me in the shadows, that the more flawed one was, the more difficult it became not merely to stick to that path but to see it as it unfurled towards that lasting happiness and fulfilment which human beings found so elusive – and indeed a perfect journey, ensured by the perfect alignment of the ego with the inner self where the immanent God dwelt, would have been difficult to imagine if Christ has not been sent to show us the way, yet there he still was, a timeless image, the man who was wholly human yet so God-centred that he was wholly divine, and he was himself the way to that kingdom of values, those absolute truths which gave all creation meaning.

Behind that paragraph lies a rich tradition: Austen Farrer, Somerset Ward, William Temple, T.S. Eliot, Dorothy L. Sayers. And behind them Lancelot Andrewes, Nicholas Ferrar, Donne and Herbert – and behind *them* Julian of Norwich, Anselm and Aquinas, Francis and Dominic, and the great fathers and mothers of faith from the first century and before. I am convinced that what will last is the worship of Jesus as the God-man, back to St Paul and St John and the great tragic divide which took Christianity out of first-century sectarian Judaism and into the world market-place.

We cannot be righteous of ourselves, says St Paul. If we were to accept this I think it might relieve some of the anxiety that weighs us down as Catholic Christians. We are not here to make nervous, defensive, moralistic judgements. Our whole way of being as Church in the world is the dangerous acceptance of humanity in all its sacredness and scarredness; it is not to moralise or be nervous or defensive in the face of so-called secularisation. It may be to accept that some of what we call secularisation is a genuine lifting of burdens on people, an opening up of sacred space in place of oppressive religious restriction.

I know there are those who believe that our culture is depraved, and who trace everything from the destruction of the rain forest to tales of naughty vicars on the loss of religious faith and the vulgarity of mass media. I have dark moods when I share that point of view. But I cannot get round the central Catholic claim of the Christian faith that God has in Christ taken on our humanity, taken us up into himself and contended for us and with us. Nothing that is human is alien to God. This is surely the message of *Gaudium et spes*, that keynote document of the Second Vatican Council which still rings down the years to us Catholic Christians of the Anglican tradition:

> The joy and the hope, the sorrow and anxiety of this age of humanity, especially of the poor and of those who are in any way suffering; these Christ's disciples make their own, and there is nothing human that does not find an echo in their hearts.

There is a cosmological claim being enacted whenever the Eucharist is celebrated and the Word of God spoken and shared. A claim that God has made humanity his own; all of us, Christian and non-Christian, believer and non-believer, insider and outsider. That is a claim to live within and to die for, not only for our own sake but for the sake of all whom the second evangelist described as 'those

6 A National Church?[1]*

John Moses

There are many for whom the discovery of Catholicism within the Church of England has been an important part of the journey of faith. This is why Affirming Catholicism matters so much. What all of us want to see is the rediscovery within our Church of a broad-based Catholicism – a Catholicism that takes seriously the story, the tradition and the experience of the Church; a Catholicism that is prepared to work at the interface between continuity and change; a Catholicism that is committed to the mission of the Church, willing to work across the boundaries of church and community life; a Catholicism that is imaginative, critical, courteous and adventurous.

It must inevitably follow that such a rediscovery cannot take place unless there are important shifts of emphasis in various areas of church life. One such area is the way in which Catholics in our Church actually look at the Church of England – its integrity, its authority, and not least its position as the national Church.

Over many generations, and sometimes for good reason, the traditional stance of Catholics within the Church of England towards its position as the national Church, the established Church, has been at best one of ambivalence, and at worst one of indifference or contempt. There have been some for whom establishment has compromised the integrity of the Church. It has been tantamount to a kind of Erastianism which subordinates the Church to the interests of the State and removes from the Church the freedom of self-development and the freedom of critical encounter that properly belong to the Church. There have been some for whom establishment has been not merely an obstacle to ecumenical dialogue, but something that is actually incompatible with an ecumenical Catholicism. And it scarcely needs to be said that the word 'establishment' distorts the debate. It is a word that speaks (or appears to speak) of a privileged status that is inappropriate for the Church, and especially in a situation in which all Churches count for little in the consciousness of many people. And yet it could be argued that a true understanding of the Catholic heritage of the Church of England requires a critical but wholehearted commitment to the role and the task of the Church of England as the national Church, a Church that exists for the sake of those who do not belong.

The integrity of the Church of England does not stand or fall by its position in law as the established Church, but by its continuing commitment to the principles of Catholicism and Reformation. The identity and the integrity of the Church of England rest upon the conviction that the model of a reformed Catholicism is fundamentally correct. The authority of the Anglican tradition will be tested ultimately by the authority of the whole Christian tradition.

So let us turn to the Christian tradition. Much is made (and rightly so) in the affirmation of our Catholic heritage of the Scriptures, the sacraments, the creeds, and the orders of ministry. It was the boast of our Anglican forefathers of the sixteenth century that, 'We have planted no new religion but only renewed the old that was undoubtedly founded and used by the apostles of Christ and other holy fathers of the primitive church.'[2] The seventeenth-century tag employed by Anglican theologians – 'one canon, two testaments, three creeds, four councils, five centuries'[3] – bore witness to the conviction that those early centuries provided the fundamentals of faith and order, the all-important threads of continuity. But those early centuries suggest other things that might take their place alongside the Scriptures, the sacraments, the creeds, and the orders of ministry, as being important parts of our Catholic heritage.

First, there was the development of a theological tradition: a tradition that was rational, systematic and apologetic; a tradition in which faith and reason were concerned to engage critically with the world. Second, there was an awareness as the Church grew and took its place in the later Roman Empire that the spiritual and the temporal are required to live in relation to each other, that Church and State are interconnected and interdependent. Third, there was as a consequence of these two things the emergence of a philosophical tradition – even a philosophy of history – that was concerned to relate human history to the purposes of God and to reconcile the Church's understanding of God and the world and humankind.

If Catholicism is by definition concerned with the wholeness of things – deeply and passionately committed to seeing life in its entirety in the light of all that it believes about God's revelation of himself in Jesus Christ – does it not follow that these things have a proper claim upon our understanding of what constitutes the formative, the defining, tradition of the early centuries? Indeed, the Scriptures, the sacraments, the creeds, and the orders of ministry make little sense unless they are set within the context of a robust theological tradition, of a profound conviction that the sacred and the secular are bound up together, and of a philosophy of history that is concerned to relate all that we believe about God to the world in which we live.

The Church inherited from the ancient world the ideal of a universal society. It would be sheer fantasy to speak today as though Church and State are one within a Christian commonwealth. But this was the great ideal that was carried forward and embodied in the English Reformation settlement. It was given its classic expression by Richard Hooker: 'There is not any man of the Church of England but the same man is also a member of the commonwealth; nor any man a member of the commonwealth which is not also of the Church of England.'[4]

The circumstances in which the Church *in* England was reshaped and re-formed as the Church *of* England in the course of the sixteenth century are well known. The Reformation was concerned with the purifying of religion. The English Reformation provided not only a religious settlement that was Catholic and reformed, but a settlement that was bound up also with questions of national identity.

Much has been made of the fact that the Church of

England chose to occupy the middle ground – to find the middle way – between the conflicting demands of Rome and Geneva. There were many sixteenth- and seventeenth-century divines for whom the meaning of the middle way was absolutely clear. It meant a continuing dialogue between Scripture, tradition *and* reason. It presupposed an appeal to the authority of the Early Fathers *and* an openness to new learning. It demanded a commitment to the historic continuity of the Catholic Church *and* to the freedom of national Churches.

But there is one other thing that ought to be said. The emphasis upon the middle way had at its heart traditions of comprehension and liberality that must also be rediscovered if the Church of England is to be true to itself. *Key words in the Anglican vocabulary are not compromise but comprehension; not liberalism but liberality.*

Quite apart from the story and the tradition, it is necessary also to have regard to our experience. The world in which we live today calls in question any idea that the establishment of religion – let alone of any one Church – can be easily defended. It is not merely the problem that is posed by the existence of separated Christian Churches alongside each other. Nor is it even the evolution of a multiracial, multifaith, society. It is far more the fact that the culture of the modern world is profoundly secular; and societies such as our own that are nominally Christian are for all practical purposes secular in thought and feeling and action. Religious institutions have suffered a loss of authority, of credibility. Religious symbols have lost their power. Religious faith is seen as little more than a matter of private choice.

Yet in spite of all these things it is important to recall that at its best the establishment principle has served Church and nation, and continues to do so. The determination of a national Church to maintain a nationwide ministry means an unequivocal commitment to communities, to institutions and to individuals. It is in the parishes – in the Church's relation to people as individuals and in its relation to the institutions of community life – that it is possible to discover the inherent strengths of a ministry that is based upon the establishment principle. It is here that ministry is worked out in the light of the story, the identity, the needs and the opportunities that present themselves. It follows that the Church of England is well qualified to understand the different degrees of association that people want and are capable of sustaining. Nothing must ever compromise the Church's call to conversion, to new life in Christ, to holiness. But let there be the grace to acknowledge the large numbers of people who are not able to stand firmly within the life of the Church, but for whom God and the Church and Christian faith mean something, and who in their inarticulate way ask that they shall not be excluded in our pastoral ministry by rigorous definitions of Church association. St Augustine of Hippo's word remains: 'Many seem to be within who are in reality without, and others seem to be without who are in reality within.'[5]

There is a great deal of cynicism today where all institutions in society are concerned, and the Church of England as the established Church cannot expect to escape unscathed. But the expectations and the opportunities that surround all of us as clergy and congregations are unique. It may well be the case that no one religious tradition – let alone any one Church – can easily or fully represent the aspirations of the whole nation, but still even in England at the end of the twentieth century there is a residual sense that the Christian religion is worthy of respect, that it is tolerant, that it holds and feeds the values that serve to unite.

Many who are not Anglicans are grateful for a continuing establishment because of the public recognition it provides of the place of religion, and especially of the Christian religion. Indeed, there is some evidence that the leaders of other faiths that are now settled in this country – over and above the members of other Christian Churches – often welcome our establishment as a means whereby the Church of England can initiate action with them or on their behalf in the public domain.

The English experience of the Church–State relationship is unique. The situation may well be anomalous. But it is not immediately self-evident that Church or State have anything to gain by removing this dimension from our common life at the present time. Such a step could so easily strengthen the drift towards sectarianism. It would undoubtedly lead to a loss of the comprehensiveness and all-inclusiveness that have been the hallmarks of the Church of England. It was Eamon Duffy, the Roman Catholic Reformation historian, who wrote that, 'Disestablishment would be in favour of nothing, the relegation of religion to the realm of the private, and the emptying of our common life of some of the values and assumptions which have shaped it for a thousand years.'[6]

But talk about establishment and what it means to be a national Church must never be allowed to lead to self-deception. The statistics of church life are a sobering reminder of the relatively small numerical base from which the churches exercise their ministry. Research carried out in England over the last six years suggests that 90 per cent of the population – over 35 million adults and 8 million children – are outside the regular worshipping life of the church as measured by church attendance.[7] And if attention is turned to the numerical yardsticks by which the life of the Church of England might be measured – Sunday attendance, the electoral roll, Easter communicants, infant baptism, confirmation and marriage – there is a pattern of substantial and continuing decline throughout much of this century.

There is in England a long-standing tradition of indifference, of unselfconscious secularism, but the Church of England has traditionally provided the framework within which the religious aspirations of non-churchgoing people might also find expression from time to time. But the point has now been reached when it has to be asked if the decline in all the numerical yardsticks of church life is not so great that the Church of England has ceased to be in any meaningful sense the Church of the nation. The Church of England might continue to be established in law, but can it claim to be established in the hearts of people?

Talk about the seriousness of our situation is not only a question of numbers. There is the problem of maintaining a nationwide parochial and stipendiary ministry. There are the ambiguities and the pain implicit in the decision to ordain women to the priesthood. There are questions of authority and the balance that is to be struck between the episcopal and the synodical systems. There are the complex ethical issues in which all of us are caught up in our relation to each other, to society, and to the environment. There are the large questions of public values and public priorities. These are not matters that only concern the interior life of the Church. They are the concern of Church and nation. They suggest that the interests of Church and State might best be served by keeping open all existing relationships. The abandonment of establishment – not merely the legal form but the expectations which it properly sustains – could so easily encourage the Church to withdraw into itself to the exclusion of that wider ministry and mission which at its best the Church has always attempted.

It is inconceivable in today's world that the Church of England will pursue its ministry in isolation. The commitment to ecumenism and to the Anglican Communion requires an openness to new insights and new developments that cannot be foreseen. The numerical weakness of the Church gives cause for concern. There is a long-standing tradition of indifference. There are influences at work in society at large which appear to demand that the Churches shall identify themselves increasingly by their separation from the world. But the relationship between Church and State – diminished, disregarded and caricatured – still represents a serious attempt to give practical and public expression to the relation of Christianity to the whole of life. The Church will always wrestle with what it means to be a community of faith; but the paradox of being the Church in the world requires that the Church will take its place in all the structures, relationships and experiences of life. Bonhoeffer's plea that God shall be found at the centre of life[8] is one that the Church of England is supremely well qualified to understand.

The intriguing question for those of us who want to explore the meaning of Catholic evangelism is whether there are things in the story, the tradition and the experience of our Church, which serve to indicate some of the ways in which we might move forward. There are, perhaps, four areas where Catholics might find that they have a distinctive contribution to make and where a serious commitment to the Church of England as the national Church might inform and shape our approach.

First, *theology*. The foundation charter of Affirming Catholicism tells of 'the conviction of many that a respect for scholarship and free enquiry has been characteristic of the Church of England and the Churches of the wider Anglican communion from the earliest times'. Scholarship and free enquiry. Yes, this is an important part of our Catholic heritage. It matters today as never before. It matters partly because of the religious fundamentalism that is to be found throughout the world, and it matters also because one of the reasons why the Christian tradition has been disregarded in recent generations in the Western world is that it is simply not seen by many people as having anything to say to their experience of living in the world. This is why one contribution that Catholics might make to evangelism is to plead for the recovery of a natural theology. Certainly, in the writings of the seventeenth-century Anglican divines it was the emphasis upon the creation and the incarnation which made them demand that all fields of knowledge should be open to scrutiny, and that account must therefore be taken of natural theology.

If our starting-point is faith seeking understanding; if it is still required that reason shall be brought into an open dialogue with Scripture and tradition; if it is acknowledged that theology cannot do its work in isolation; if there is a willingness to work across all the boundaries of academic life; then it might be possible to recover over the generations an awareness of what theology – Christian theology – can contribute to our understanding of God and the world and humankind.

This is why there are some for whom it was not the Tractarians but the contributors to Lux Mundi who were the true successors to the seventeenth-century Anglican divines. There was in their writings the commitment to engagement and dialogue that has always been an important part of the Church's apologetic work. There is ground to be recovered, but it is possible to present the claims of a revealed religion by drawing upon our experience of the world and the interpretation of the human mind.

Archbishop Michael Ramsey spoke of the great Christian

centuries to come.[9] It is impossible for us to know if Christian theology can ever be seen again as the queen of the sciences. But our theological method – quite literally the way we do theology as Anglicans – suggests to me that here is one area where Catholics – above all Catholics – might make a contribution.

Second, *prayer*. In the tradition of the Orthodox Church the theologian is one who follows the path of union with God.[10] The disciplines of theology and prayer cannot be detached from each other. 'The true science of God is that which leads us to love God.'[11] Whatever else the Tractarians were about, they restored to the English Church an awareness of the transcendence of God and of the mystery of God's revelation. They became associated in the public mind with ritual, with the enrichment of public worship, with the introduction of liturgical ceremonies that owed much to the Roman tradition. But above everything else they represented a rediscovery of the Church's call to holiness, of the disciplined life, of personal piety, and of new standards of pastoral ministry. But what does it mean today to Catholics in the Church of England – committed to evangelism – to rediscover the Church's call to holiness?

'Every scribe who has been trained for the kingdom of heaven is like a householder who brings out of his treasure what is new and what is old' (RSV).[12] There is a word that speaks to me of Catholicism and Reformation, of continuity and change. Let us look briefly at public worship and private prayer.

Public worship. Is it not the case that the busyness of so much church life today is reflected in worship, with its emphasis upon self-conscious forms of participation? It is not merely that we have lost in many places any sense of mystery, of transcendence. It is far more that we have forgotten the anonymity that many people require as they approach God in worship. There are large numbers of people for whom the experience of God is tentative, fragmented, elusive. But they want to be there. And in any case, there is more than one kind of participation. It is not always possible to be exuberant, frenetic. Christians cannot be alleluia people all the time! There is the very serious danger of losing a tradition of public prayer that is not merely ordered and dignified, but also reflective and contemplative, giving people the space in which they can make their own connections, find their own interpretations, but all within the context of common prayer. Here surely are things that Catholics in the Church of England are able to understand.

And private prayer. It was an Orthodox priest visiting England at the time of the World Partners in Mission exercise in the 1980s who remarked of the Church of England that, 'This Church needs a lot of prayer and fasting and silence and solitude.' Our generation has had to discover the limitations of words and the depths, the riches, of silence. One modern writer who stands in the tradition of desert spirituality says that, 'Not every Christian can or should live as a hermit. But every Christian must have an inner hermitage in which to meet his God.'[13] The desert – not as a place but as an inescapable experience – has much to teach us. The emptiness and the poverty that are felt by all of us in the life of prayer might be demanding that we rediscover the desert tradition with its emphasis upon solitude, testing, self-emptying, encounter and transfiguration.

The story is told of a man who came to Abba Joseph, one of the early Desert Fathers, and said, 'Father, according as I am able, I keep my little rule, and my little fast, my prayer and meditation and contemplative silence; and according as I am able, I strive to cleanse my heart of thoughts: now, what more should I do?' The elder rose up in reply, stretched out his hands to heaven and his fingers became like ten lamps of fire. He said, 'Why not be totally changed into fire?'[14] Transfiguration – yes. But perhaps our generation must first learn to go into the darkness of solitude, testing, self-emptying and encounter. And to those who ask, 'What does this have to do with evangelism?' the answer has to be, 'Unless a wheat grain falls on the ground and dies, it remains only a single grain; but if it dies, it yields a rich harvest.'[15]

Third, *ministry*. The Church is called to be a sign of the Kingdom of God. But it is also patently plain that the Church is required to live in an open relationship with society. It may well prove to be the case that Church and

State in England have entered a transitional phase. There is a post-establishment culture in which the religious conventions of public life are easily disregarded. But if the Church is to remain serviceable and accessible, then account must be taken of the wider constituencies of faith and feeling that surround all our churches. Let us acknowledge the inarticulate religion of those who do not stand exactly where we stand but for whom God still counts for something. It is important to meet the needs of communities and institutions and individuals for celebration and ritual and symbol. It was a seventeenth-century Puritan divine who remarked that it is the task of the Church of England to tolerate the tolerable.[16] There are pressures both within society and the Church that are erecting clear boundary fences. That cannot be right. Let us plead on the basis of Catholic convictions for a Church that leaves many doors open by which many people might find their way home.

But even while we set our faces firmly against the sectarianism and the congregationalism that are to be found in too many places, let critical thought be given to a strategy for ministry that takes account of the pastoral facts of life as we experience them. And this is another place where Catholics might also have an important contribution to make. Henry Chadwick reminded us that a Church that has lost its memory has become a geriatric Church. One of the things that we desperately lack in so many areas of life today is a historical perspective. Is this not something that Catholics might bring? It is only *a* suggestion, but it is worth remembering that behind the parish church system, which presupposes a settled population that is basically Christian and basically church-going, there lies the minster church system which might be more appropriate in an age that is required to take very seriously the missionary situation in which we now find ourselves. None of us would make any apology for our commitment to parochial ministry and all that it represents, but let there also be an awareness of the need to identify the strong centres of church life from which the Church's ministry might be taken out. These will be the centres – and not necessarily the ancient centres – that are unashamedly in the business of worship, of Christian formation, of community involvement, of evangelism. It might well be that the minster church tradition provides a way forward that is consistent with our story as a Church.

Fourth, *social action*. It is a commonplace that evangelism must always have for Catholics a social dimension. Here again there are things within our experience as the national Church that might helpfully point us in certain directions.

There is a corporate dimension that can never be excluded from our thinking as we try to work our way through some of the complex issues with which we all wrestle. The world understands all too well the tug-of-war between authority and freedom, between corporate responsibility and personal autonomy. And so does the Church – not least of all the Church of England! It is, after all, in the Scriptures, tested at every point by our experience of life, that we find the distinctively Catholic emphasis that questions of personal freedom and personal responsibility must always be set within the wider understanding of the corporate nature of our community, of the corporate personality in which we share, of the inescapable connection between the well-being of a people and the faith by which it lives.

There is also a prophetic tradition with which Catholics (but not only Catholics) have rightly been associated down the generations. I share the doubts of those who wonder whether it is possible for the Church as an institution to be prophetic. What does matter, however, is that the Church as an institution should give to individuals – clergy and lay people alike – the freedom in which some will find the call to be prophets in their day. This is why the freedom of our Church – the freedom it gives to clergy and congregations – seems to me to be so precious. It is essentially something to do with the Church giving its children something of the freedom that God gives to his creation – the freedom to be, to do, and to become. It is one of the happy paradoxes that, although we are the national Church, the established Church, we have this freedom to a far greater degree than any other Church in Christendom – and it is a freedom to be used!

Catholic evangelism is the theme of this conference.

Catholicism and the national Church is the subject of this chapter. The subject speaks of the conviction that there are things within the story, the tradition and the experience of the Church of England which Catholics might properly draw upon as they take their part in the Church's work of evangelism. It has seemed right to point in four directions – theology, prayer, ministry and social action – but what has mattered most of all has been the conviction that there are things that properly belong to our Catholic heritage that are to be found within our experience as a national Church. It was Percy Dearmer, writing nearly a hundred years ago, who said, 'I do love the Church of England so much. She might be what no other Church in Christendom is. I believe she could even still be, if she came right off her pedestal ... and laid her treasures at the feet of the poor.' Our Church has been humbled a good deal since those words were written, but there ought to be no doubt about the treasures that are still possessed and that might yet enable us to be what no other Church in Christendom is.

There is a tradition of sound learning which is informed and renewed by the disciplines of scripture, tradition and reason. There is a tradition of practical divinity which has repeatedly found expression in a positive endorsement of the voluntary principle. There is a tradition of thoughtful, earthy, unselfconscious holiness. There is a tradition of comprehension, of liberality, which has enabled the Church to offer public ministry with courtesy and generosity.

And these traditions, these treasures, continue to find expression in patterns of ministry that are rooted in theological convictions that lie at the heart of our faith. They are patterns of ministry that are rooted in the life of the local community. They are patterns of ministry that are related to individuals and institutions without regard to church membership or church attendance as prior conditions of ministry.

These patterns presuppose a commitment to God in his creation; a commitment to the fundamental principle of incarnation; a commitment to the transcendent dimension of grace in all situations and relationships. If these patterns, these commitments, can be held on to, then it might still

95

be possible to move towards Archbishop William Temple's great ideal of the Church as the one institution that exists for the sake of those who do not belong.

Notes

1 The writing of this paper has drawn in part upon John Moses, *A Broad and Living Way*, The Canterbury Press, 1995.

2 Cited by Henry McAdoo, 'Richard Hooker', in Geoffrey Rowell (ed.), *The English Religious Tradition and the Genius of Anglicanism*, Ikon, 1992, p. 108.

3 Cited by Henry McAdoo, *The Spirit of Anglicanism*, A & C Black, 1965, p. 320.

4 Richard Hooker, *Of the Laws of Ecclesiastical Polity*, VIII, 1.2.

5 Cited by Yves M.-J. Congar, *The Mystery of the Temple*, Burnes & Oates, 1962, p. 197.

6 Eamon Duffy, *The Tablet*, 22 January 1994.

7 Peter Brierley, *Christian England*, MARC Europe, 1991.

8 Dietrich Bonhoeffer, *Letters and Papers from Prison*, SCM, 1971.

9 Christopher Martin (ed.), *The Great Christian Centuries To Come: Essays in Honour of A.M. Ramsey*, Mowbray, 1974, p. 1.

10 Vladimir Lossky, *The Mystical Theology of the Eastern Church*, James Clarke, 1957, p. 39.

11 Jean Daniélou, *God and Us* (trans. by Walter Roberts), Mowbray, 1957, p. 171.

12 Matthew 13:52.

13 A Monk, *The Hermitage Within*, Darton, Longman & Todd, 1977.

14 Abbott Joseph of Panephysis, cited by Thomas Merton, *The Wisdom of the Desert*, Sheldon Press, 1974, p. 50.

15 John 12:24.

16 Cited by H. H. Henson, *Retrospect of an Unimportant Life*, vol. I (1863–1920), OUP, 1942, pp. 305–6.

Postscript: Talk of the Devil*

Rowan Williams

One of the things you do when you get baptised is to repudiate the devil. I am glad to know that the Liturgical Commission has been busily reintroducing some fairly robust language about this. Talk of the devil is so often these days a bit coy or a bit comical, a bit embarrassing or a bit camp, at least among right-thinking (affirming) sorts of people; it is the kind of thing surely best left to those peculiar charismatics that right-thinking people are so snooty about. But this is rather a pity. If we are encouraging folk to turn their backs on the devil (even if not actually to spit on him, as in a more liturgically uninhibited age), we had better have *some* notion of what, other than a stale joke, he actually is (I say 'he' in the hope that, for once, the non-inclusive language may be allowed to stand).

Let us first get out of the way a possible objection: the charge that talk of the devil is negative, depressing, a legacy of those sad days when people believed they needed redeeming from something, or held that creation was bad for you; that it is not an appropriate subject for what should be an upbeat occasion, or for an age recovering 'original blessing' or whatever. A fair objection in one way, I suppose. Devil language can be used and has been used to reinforce a sense of the alienation between the world, the soul and God and to intensify a certain sense of gloom about the risks of getting created at all. But before we pack the devil off to the offices of whatever overworked heavenly therapist is sorting out the neuroses of the Church Fathers, we should stop and recognise some of the force and vision in the myth – and its profoundly positive under-

*© Rowan Williams 1996

tow. Talk of the devil says that the present state of things is not how it *has* to be; the source of the worst pain and horror is not, after all, some iron necessity, but an eruption of avoidable and therefore, in the long run, *healable* destructiveness. It says that the choice of evil or darkness is against the grain of things and so ultimately ridiculous: the devil knows, better than we do, what creation is all about and says no to it – which means saying yes to chaos and emptiness, to your own nothingness. We are not made for nonsense like this, sawing off the branch we are sitting on; when we say yes to chaos, violence, destruction, we are being as 'unnatural', as insane, as Lucifer.

There is a good solid theological tradition that sees the devil as, in effect, mad. Not *stupid*, exactly. Indeed, if you look at his triumphs in human history, absolutely brilliant in certain respects; but still – you can see the familiar glint in the eye, the look of someone determined to think what they like ('don't confuse me with facts'). The devil's rebellion against God is evil stripped to the basics: no bad habits, no original sin, no inadequate parenting to appeal to, just the tiny, raw element of saying no to reality. When we want to think seriously about sin, we could do worse than test for the presence of this element, this bare refusal of truth. There is a lot of it about.

But this is where talk of the devil begins to impinge on evangelism. The Gospel of Jesus Christ is contact with reality, as direct as the contact of water with a dry throat. The devil has an immense vested interest in his version of reality and is eager that we should not come into contact with Christ's truth; so he works to make and to keep us untruthful. And if he can make the very act of sharing the Gospel itself an evasion of the truth, so much the better for him. What he will most dislike is the sort of experience that jolts us into touch with reality.

Incidentally, these ambitious claims to know how the devil's mind works should not be taken as merely picturesque meanderings. Of course, I do not know any more than you do *what* exactly the devil is; it is all too easy to laugh off the familiar pictures. But thinking about the devil is looking into and *beyond* our own compulsive untruthfulness, trying to confront our own no-saying in its depths.

As C. S. Lewis said about Milton's imagining of Satan in *Paradise Lost*, all we have to do is to project just a little from what we already know of ourselves, to refine the essence of our own evil; and to admit that the energy of our no-saying is a bit more than just the sum total of human cussedness, that there is something beyond our individual evasions.

Anyway – what are some of the devil's likes and dislikes? Well, he is very fond of anxiety, the more extreme and over-the-top the merrier. Evangelism that springs from anxiety ('O - God-how-are-we-going-to-pay-our-bills-if-we-haven't-got-any-people? anxiety, for instance, or 'How-the-hell-do-I-know-I'm-right-if-there-are people-who-don't-agree-with-me?' anxiety) is a gift to him. So is evangelism that sets out to induce anxiety ('Shouldn't-you-be-panicking-about-what-happens-when-you-die?'). Churches that live in per-petual anxiety are wonderful for the devil's purposes – anxiety about purity, about survival, about too much compromise or too little, about conservation, about inno-vation, whatever. Anxiety is always a subtle exercise in the courting of unreality, the repeated shaping of the world into a monstrous agenda that *I* am supposed to sort out.

But here is the paradox. The devil loves anxiety, but he hates *fear*. There is a fine short story by Doris Lessing about an extraterrestrial mission to earth which finally (despairingly) reports back that, 'These are creatures with a deficient sense of fear.' We are not afraid enough of our capacity to say no: to devastate our environment; to plan and work systematically for mass murder by the manufac-ture of nightmare weapons; to trade in these obscenities and pretend it is a minor and neutral bit of business; to tolerate a massive level of public evasiveness and lying in these and many other areas. Here we *should* be afraid – not anxious in the face of problems, but afraid in the face of the horror and lies that threaten our moral substance as human beings.

Afraid, too, of our ability to collude in the wastage of generations by unemployment and educational wreckage, afraid of how quickly we can learn to live with poverty, apathy and injustice, and afraid of the cruelty and selfish-ness we bring to our relations with each other. We spend so much time struggling to emphasise the goodness of sexuality (understandably, given the Christian record on this) that we can forget to be afraid here too of the terrible energies of unreality. And above all we had better be afraid of our Christian capacity to slither past all this and utter easy words about it. They may be the easy words of fundamentalism; they may just as well be the easy words of a liberal niceness unwilling to be really frightened by evil within and without. The devil has a soft spot for theology; I think he also watches reports, resolutions, synods, Lambeth Conferences (and probably Affirming Catholic events now, as well) with a fair bit of sympathetic interest, to precisely the extent that they embody no real fear.

Because if we do not know about this, then we do not know what it is to hear Jesus saying, 'Fear not', as he so often does. In Jesus's ministry, the coming horrors of the birthpangs of the new age are spelt out with clarity; and *then*, 'Fear not' becomes a serious and a joyful word, becomes Good News. *Look* at the coming darkness, in detail, without flinching, says Jesus: *then* you may understand what God is saying. Not that you will necessarily be spared or rescued; simply that what you are is held, welcomed and sustained by the world's maker. You are loved and you are not destroyed, and you are made alive in the one in whom all things hold together. Tibetan Buddhists train novices in visualising frightful apparitions that will lacerate and dismember them: only then do they know that their total vulnerability is both inescapable *and* not the ultimately important thing. Beyond it is the causeless compassion that arises when fear has been faced, named and lived through. Christians should have some idea of what is going on here. The devil says, 'Don't be afraid; be *anxious*; panic.' When told, 'Don't panic,' we would happily endorse the words of the great Basil (Fawlty): 'What else is there to do?' But Jesus says, '*Don't* be anxious; meet your proper fears; then let go and fear no more.' Repent, he says, go down into the death and dissolution we all dread; be baptised.

If that is right, the Good News is expressed most simply in a style of life that teaches honestly about what is to be feared, the possibilities and realities of corruption, the ways we become used to getting on top of our situation by glib talk. A style of life, too, that realises the sustaining welcome of God, the anchorage of our reality, past, present and future, in the life of God, whose fullness is more and more being uncovered *for* us and *in* us. And here is one place where the *Catholic* evangelist has a specific and vital contribution. Put too much emphasis on how to actualise this reconciled style of life and you are back with either anxiety or evasion, with the endless struggle to get it right, or the rather nervous and aggressive confidence that we *have* got it right, never mind the casualties along the road and don't you *dare* suggest otherwise. Put too much emphasis on the utter independence of God's work and our innate uselessness, and you end up incapable of taking risks, and so never confronting *real* fear and *real* failure. But against these distortions, moralist and pietist, the Catholic tradition affirms that the life of God and God's Kingdom is real and concrete here, not in our achievement but in the sacraments. *There* is the steady course run by divine reality in our midst, the life and death and resurrection of Jesus, into which our lives are invited, so that they weave in and out of that solid and central history – and sometimes are so drawn in, woven in, that they become a kind of sacrament themselves.

When we can see this at the heart, the steady accessibility of the God who is *there* in these symbolic events of death and re-creation, of breaking and feeding, we have that much more freedom to look at fear and darkness and to allow ourselves to confront failure. We are able to risk saying things, doing things, in the name of Jesus, knowing their vulnerability, their potential and real corruption, because the inviting, transforming presence will survive our betrayals of it. We dare to preach at the Eucharist because the act that makes the Eucharist is more than our words and can take to itself and live through yet another shipwreck of ideas and hopes.

To move in and out of this sacramental solidity is thus also to move in and out of silence; to let the words be absorbed in the doing (God's doing), in the history that is not just ours, in the divine humanity among us. The devil does not like silence, especially not the silence that points

101

to the living Word. The devil does not like the silence when we recognise the emptiness or distortedness of what we have just said; or the silence of waiting for words to come, rather than rushing into saving formulae. All these silences are alive with good news, with the *givenness* of the Word among us, in flesh, in water, in bread and wine, in words of forgiveness and promises of faithfulness. From such silence we find freedom to look outwards, to move out of the religious ghetto (always a good soil for anxiety) and to name what we fear – the cowardice and glibness in us, the violence and impenitence in us and the world. If Christ lives on the far side of honest fear, pass over to him there; from there comes the preaching of the Gospel. At the empty tomb, 'They said nothing ... for they were afraid'; but beyond their fear and their silence, the Word of God rose up like the dawn, steadily and irresistibly.

What does the devil love? Anxiety, chatter, lying, fantasy. Why should he have what he likes?

Do you turn to Christ? I turn to Christ.

Do you renounce Satan? I renounce Satan.